Fiscal Centralization and Tax Burdens:

State and Regional Financing of City Services

Fiscal Centralization and Tax Burdens:

State and Regional Financing of City Services

Roy W. Bahl
Walter Vogt

Metropolitan Studies Program
The Maxwell School
Syracuse University

The research and studies forming the
basis for this report were conducted
prusuant to a contract between the
Department of Housing and Urban
Development and the National League
of Cities.

Ballinger Publishing Company ● **Cambridge, Mass.**
A Subsidiary of J.B. Lippincott Company

Copyright © 1975 by Ballinger Publishing Company. All rights reserved. No part of this publication may be reproduced, stored in a retrieval system, or transmitted in any form or by any means, electronic mechanical photocopy, recording or otherwise, without the prior written consent of the publisher.

International Standard Book Number: 0-88410-423-0

Library of Congress Catalog Card Number: 75-31649

Printed in the United States of America

Library of Congress Cataloging in Publication Data

Bahl, Roy W
    Fiscal centralization and tax burdens,

    1. Municipal finance—United States—Case studies. 2. Intergovernmental fiscal relations—United States—Case Studies. 3. Intergovernmental tax relations—United States—Case studies.
    I. Vogt, Walter, 1943- joint author. II. Title.
    HJ9145.B28   353.007'25   75-31649
    ISBN 0-88410-423-0

Contents

List of Tables and Figures

Preface

This study is the outgrowth of the Urban Observatory Municipal Finance Research Project on the equity implications of state and regional government financial assumption of city government functions. As such, this report is a compilation and synthesis of intensive case studies carried out in nine cities—Atlanta; Boston; Denver; Baltimore; San Diego; Nashville; Milwaukee; Kansas City, Kansas; and Kansas City, Missouri—under this program. The intent in these studies is to fill a major gap in knowledge about the proper assignment of functions between levels of government—the uncertainty about the equity implications of alternative financing schemes. We attempt to do this by providing hard evidence on the tax burden implications of state financial assumption and the creation of region-wide financing districts.

This research in no way substitutes for the underlying case studies. Each case study is careful and detailed, and a full appreciation of the results and the policy implications for each city can only be had from a study of each volume. What we do here is to combine the results of these studies, to generalize the findings, and to draw out the policy implications of such generalizations.

The aim of this research is to improve the process of formulating public policies about urban governance. Accordingly, these studies were carried out in conjunction with city government officials, with an eye always toward studying only workable and politically feasible reform measures. Hopefully a consequence of this real-world view is that the policy guidance suggested in these results will be of practical use. Another intended virtue of this set of case studies, which might make it different from predecessors, is the comparability of the approach taken and therefore of the results obtained. The data used, the income concept, the shifting assumptions, and the simple simulation model were all standardized to insure comparability. However, care was taken to insure that these standardizations in no way impeded the capturing of the circumstances of individual cities.

The Metropolitan Studies Program of the Maxwell School served institutionally in the direction and coordination of this project. In large part we were responsible for the standardization discussed above. The income concept used was developed jointly by us and a committee of researchers from the Observatories: Professor William Oakland of Ohio State University, Professor Kenneth Hubbell of the University of Missouri at Kansas City, and Professors Larry Schroeder and David Sjoquist of Georgia State University. Most of the original work on the concept and the leadership of the committee belonged to Professor Oakland.

We are indebted to many for the completion of this work. Sheldon Mann and Marsha Weissman served ably as graduate research assistants in the early stages of the project, Lawrence Williams and William Barnes of the National League of Cities provided assistance at every turn, and our colleagues in the Maxwell School—particularly Alan Campbell and Seymour Sacks—made a number of helpful suggestions for revision of this manuscript. Finally, there is our debt to Melanie Cook, Mary D'Archangel, Cecilia Resti, and Nancye Yacher who patiently typed and edited the manuscript. Despite all of this assistance, responsibility for the conclusions here is ours alone.

Roy W. Bahl
Walter Vogt

Chapter One

Introduction

This book is about one alternative available for resolving the considerable fiscal problems facing local governments in large central cities—the alternative of fiscal centralization. Specifically, the concern in this work is with what happens to the fiscal position of the central-city government and to tax burdens of core-city residents in different income classes when the financing of locally provided services is assumed by the state government, or by a regional government. Accordingly, the primary research issue is estimation and explanation of the budgetary and tax burden effects of certain forms of fiscal centralization. Since the governmental budgetary effects of such government reform are relatively easily worked out, the major contribution here is an empirical study of those tax burden changes that are likely to result from reassignment of financing of specified functions.

The policy implications of these results are of considerable importance. Most advocates of fiscal centralization—particularly the state assumption version—note the regressivity of local tax systems and simply assume that state or regional government financial assumption will result in city government budget relief, a more equitable distribution of tax burdens among families in different income classes, and absolute tax relief for the urban poor. The conceptual and empirical work here suggests that the problem is far too complicated to warrant such an assumption. Indeed, one clear result of this study is that while the effects vary widely between cities, tax burden *increases* may well be the result of state or regional government financial assumption of city services. From these results, however, it is possible to identify the conditions under which state (regional) government financial assumption has favorable tax burden effects on the urban poor. Out of such identification grows the major policy implications of this research.

APPROACH AND METHOD

The analysis of the income-distribution effects of reassigning financial responsibility requires three distinct steps. First, an appropriate notion of income must be developed and justified in the context of the analysis. Second, a set of assumptions about the incidence of the taxes involved and about the effects of shifting[a] on the level of expenditure for the function in question must be adopted. Finally, the empirical analysis must be carried out using these assumptions and the income concept adopted.

Similarly, the analysis of the budgetary effects of shifting requires: (1) estimation of the amount of resources freed-up as a result of financial assignment; and (2) some judgment about the extent to which these freed resources will find their way into tax reduction or will simply be viewed as monies now available to support other functions.

The focus in this research is the central city, its overlapping governments, and its residents. The empirical and conceptual analysis is based on the results of case studies carried out in nine central cities in the Urban Observatory network[b1]. The most important feature of this research design, and the credibility of the policy implications that result, is the comparative case study approach. Not only does such an approach permit an assessment of the effects of state/regional financial assumption under differing circumstances, but it insures that the peculiarities of each case city are taken into account and that the reforms proposed are feasible—politically, administratively, and fiscally—in the context of that city. In short, such results provide a useful and real-world evaluation of the financial centralization option.[2]

To achieve comparability among the nine participating cities, the basic study approach was standardized in three important respects. First, a comprehensive income concept was developed, and estimated by income class for each central city.[3] With only slight modification, all participating cities used these estimates. Second, the tax incidence assumptions and the methods of estimating the distribution of tax burdens were agreed upon and generally followed in all studies.[c] Third, the model used to simulate the overall effects of state/regional assumption was developed centrally and applied in all case studies.

In order to insure that the state/regional financial assumption plans considered were relevant to the fiscal and political realities of the cities involved,

---

[a]Throughout this study, we use the term "shifting" to refer to the reassigning of financial responsibility for any given function.

[b]The Urban Observatory cities participating in this study are Atlanta; Baltimore; Boston; Nashville-Davidson; Denver; Milwaukee; Kansas City, Kansas; Kansas City, Missouri; and San Diego.

[c]Individual cities did vary some assumptions and estimating procedures in order to conform more with local conditions, though in most cases these variations do not affect the comparability of the analysis and results. The case study descriptions in Chapters 4 and 5 below spell out these variations in some detail.

each observatory city chose its own package of candidate functions, taxes, and expenditure-level consequences. One result of this local option—the choice by some cities to consider packages of subfunctions for shifting—adds a new dimension to research on the proper assignment of functions. At the same time, these studies reinforce the contention that education, and to some extent welfare financing, remain at the very heart of the urban fiscal problem.

LIMITATIONS

This study is limited in three important respects: the jurisdictional unit studied, the range of taxes considered in the shifting process, and the tax incidence assumptions made.

With respect to the jurisdictional unit only the tax burden effects on central-city residents and budgetary implications for central-city governments are estimated. While the particularly acute fiscal problems of the central cities and their mounting concentrations of poor families in some ways justifies this focus, many important issues—such as what happens to local government budgets and taxpayers in the rest of the state—are not considered in any detail. Probably a great deal more policy use could be made of these results if the effects on all residents in a state or a region could be identified. However, because of resource limitations, such an inclusive analysis was not possible.[d]

A second limitation is that the full range of state/local taxes is not considered in analysis of the revenue adjustments that accompany financial centralization. A more elaborate empirical model might incorporate consideration of all state and all local taxes and nontax revenues, thus allowing for any tax or combinations of taxes to be used in the estimation of tax burden changes. Most of these case studies incorporate consideration of only three taxes—sales, income, and property. This assumption—that states, on average, would go to their major revenue sources for increased resources—would not seem a bad approximation.[e] Moreover, the taxes considered were chosen on the basis of what local researchers thought to be feasible alternatives.

A further set of limitations arises because of the assumptions made about the incidence of taxes. This research generally follows the conventional assumptions incorporated in previous studies: income taxes are borne by recipients, residential property taxes by owner-occupiers or renters in line with their housing consumption, and nonresidential property taxes and sales taxes by consumers at large. This provides a set of estimates that represents one extreme in tax incidence theory.

---

[d]Each city observatory was financed to study only that city and, even so, completion of the work tended to run one year behind contract schedules.

[e]Sales, income, and property taxes account for about 60 percent of total state and local government revenues.

There are conflicting views, particularly about the incidence of the property tax, and the "new view" is that the property tax is borne by owners of capital and, therefore, may actually be a progressive tax.[4] These assumptions, particularly about property tax incidence, set the extremes within which the true tax burden effects of fiscal centralization must fall. No attempt is made here to extend, or to evaluate, the theoretical debate on the incidence of the property tax, or even to compare the incidence results under different assumptions.[5] Rather, each observatory staff took a position on the issue. Of the nine cities studied, the conventional assumption was chosen as appropriate in eight cases.[f]

PLAN OF STUDY

There are three parts to this book: the setting for the analysis of financial reassignment of selecting functions (Chapters 2 and 3); the case study methodology and results (Chapters 4, 5, and 6); and the comparison of results and discussion of policy implications (Chapters 7 and 8). Chapter 2 sets the stage for this analysis by describing the shifting alternative in a context of the urban fiscal problem, and by reviewing the literature that purports to evaluate fiscal centralization. Chapter 3 presents a description of the relative economic and fiscal positions of the ten cities studied.

The concern in Chapter 4 is with the choice of functions to be considered for shifting. In Chapter 5 we describe the method used to estimate tax burdens by family size and income level, and present the results of such estimation for the nine cities. Chapter 6 begins with a presentation of the complete shifting model and then goes on to summarize the results of the individual case studies.

Chapters 7 and 8 constitute the comparative and policy implications sections of the work. Here we focus on explaining similarities and differences in the results obtained and on identifying the conditions under which state/regional assumption is likely to give better results.

NOTES

1. A similar study for New York City may be found in Chapter 5 of Roy W. Bahl, Alan K. Campbell, and David Greytak, *Taxes, Expenditures,*

---

[f]Only Arthur Becker, who directed the Milwaukee study departed from the full forward shifting assumption. He assumed that the land portion of the property tax could be estimated and would be borne by owners of capital. William Oakland, who directed the Baltimore study, is an advocate of the Harberger-Mieszkowski-McLure analysis on a national level, but still chose the conventional assumptions for the Baltimore study. He did so on grounds that the local property tax institution yields results different from those of a hypothetical national property tax of the Harberger-Mieszkowski-McLure analysis. Oakland's statement fairly summarizes the position taken in the eight case studies where the conventional or "old" view was adopted.

and the Economic Base: A Case Study of New York City (New York: Praeger Publishers, 1974).

2. Other sets of case studies of metropolitan fiscal problems and available policy options have proved useful in identifying the range of issues to be considered. However, detailed *comparative* analysis has not been attempted. Notable among these case-study compendia are Committee for Economic Development, *Fiscal Issues in the Future of Federalism,* Supplementary Paper No. 23 (New York: Committee for Economic Development, May 1968); and Advisory Commission on Intergovernmental Relations, *Fiscal Balance in the American Federal System,* Vol. 2 (Washington, D.C.: ACIR, 1967).

3. For a discussion of this income concept, see Roy Bahl and Walter Vogt, "The Fiscal Implications of Centralization," Working Paper No. 17, Maxwell Research Project on the Public Finances of New York City, Metropolitan Studies Program, Syracuse University, 1973.

4. The so-called HMM (Harberger-McLure-Mieszkowski) model—the basis of the new view—is summarized in George Break, "The Incidence and Effects of Taxation," in the *Economics of Public Finance* (Washington, D.C.: Brookings, 1974), pp. 119–240; and is applied specifically to the property tax in Peter Mieszkowski, "The Property Tax: An Excise Tax or Profits Tax," *Journal of Public Economics* (April 1972): 73–96.

5. A comparison of the tax burden effects when varying assumptions are made, on a nationwide basis, is made in Joseph Pechman and Benjamin Okner, *Who Bears the Tax Burden* (Washington, D.C.: Brookings, 1974). The debate is covered in an interesting set of papers presented at the 1973 American Economics Association meetings, "The Property Tax:Progressive or Regressive," *American Economic Review,* (May 1974): 212–235.

Chapter Two

The Case for Financial Assumption: Efficiency, Equity, and Cost Implications

The case for state or regional government financial assumption is not easily made. The arguments, pro and con, are complicated and controversial, and the issue begs for more research. In this chapter we do little more than to bare and critique these arguments. An appropriate beginning is an outlining of the nature of the urban fiscal problem and its development.

THE URBAN FISCAL PROBLEM

The much studied fiscal problems of American cities have been attributed to a multiplicity of factors,[1] including the resource implications of a declining economic base, the expenditure implications of a heavy concentration of high-cost citizens, antiquated public infrastructure, suburban exploitation, and more recently, to inflation and the bargaining successes of public employee trade unions. Whatever the underlying factors, the metropolitan fiscal problem remains severe. The imbalance between central-city expenditure needs and public resources available to meet these needs, and the disparity in service levels and tax burdens between cities and their suburbs, are large and appear to be growing.

Since the early warnings about a growing central-city fiscal problem appeared in the fifties, it has been recognized that major contributing factors are fragmented metropolitan government structure, which effectively prohibits an allocation of public resources according to expenditure needs, and a service overburden on central-city governments, that is, an imbalance between governmental expenditures required and financial resources available. While the former is more purely a local government problem, the latter relates to an "improper" balance between state-regional-local government expenditure responsibility. In recent years the problem has been accentuated by cost pressures resulting from various combinations of the catch-up of municipal wages and benefits, and inflation: property taxes do not respond to inflation as rapidly as do expenditures, municipal employee wage levels may have passed their private sector counterparts, there is little evidence of productivity increase in the public sector, and future retirement cost commitments may produce the greatest strain of all on municipal budgets. There is little doubt but that the situation will continue to worsen.

The overall response to the urban fiscal problem has been varied, and at one time or another the reform initiative has been taken by all levels of government. Through the fifties, there was still some population growth and construction activity in most central cities and hence some income elasticity to the local property tax. Assessment improvements and discretionary rate changes helped keep city fiscal positions buoyant. In the fifties and sixties, local resources were augmented by a proliferation of federal and state aid programs, and increased fund allocation under both.[a] In the sixties, central-city governments diversified their tax structures and turned to local sales and income taxes in an effort to increase revenues. Moreover, there were a number of government reform measures designed to capture regional tax bases and to provide services on an areawide basis, such as the creation of special districts, some consolidations, and a baker's dozen metropolitan governments. In the later sixties, the magnitude of local nonproperty tax revenue yield and restrictions on increased discretionary tax actions resulted in a trend toward increased state government involvement—through direct assumption and increased aids. Federal revenue-sharing has picked up a fraction of the continuing shortfall of urban government resources in the early seventies. Still, cities continue to face a severe financing constraint, now compounded by inflation-induced cost pressures. In very recent years, particularly city governments have resorted to increasing use of financial management gimmicks to improve their short-term cash flow position. Among the more prominent of these are the heavy use of short-term debt, the underfunding of retirement system programs, and the reclassification of expenditures (e.g. some current expenditures to the capital budget) to avoid tax limits. Most recently, and having exhausted all other possibilities, some city governments are turning to last-resort actions—cutting out public programs, postponing capital expenditures, and finally the laying off of public employees. The present New York City financial problems suggest that even this last resort actions may not be enough.

If one accepts the thesis that service levels in the public sector are proportional to the number of public employees,[2] the seriousness of these last-resort actions becomes clear. The implication is for an absolute deterioration of central-city services, even more inducement for suburban flight, a worsening of city social problems, and, in general, further reason for central-city decline.

Reform is imperative in such a setting. The continued fiscal dilemma of city governments—particularly those with concentrations of the poor—and the continued existence of vast disparities in service levels and tax burdens, give

---

[a]Between 1964 and 1970, the number of federal aid programs increased from 400 to 1,000, and total allocation grew from $10.141 billion to $23.954 billion.

some evidence that past reforms have not cut to the heart of the problem. Hence the issue is the nature of such new reforms. Whatever that might be, it must address the problem of central-city decline by dealing with the twin issues of intrametropolitan fiscal disparities and the functional overburden of local governments, and particularly it must raise service levels and reduce tax burdens on the urban poor.

Metropolitan Tax Burden and Expenditure Disparities

Clearly, the present-day urban fiscal problem is more severe for central-city governments than for suburban governments. A pattern of disparities in public service levels and tax burdens is a seemingly permanent fiscal characteristic of metropolitan America and an important dimension of the urban fiscal problem. The effects of today's financial emergencies will almost certainly be to widen these existing disparities and further accelerate central-city decline.

The typical pattern is one of a core city having a more severe resources-requirement gap, a lower level of public services—particularly education services—and a higher tax burden than the surrounding suburban governments. These relative differences are at least some evidence of the severity of the urban fiscal problem.

Documentation of these disparities is no easy task, since information on total state and local government fiscal activity in central-city and suburban areas are not available from published data. Therefore, certain assumptions must be made before city-suburb expenditures and tax differences can be estimated. For example, in the case of many large county governments of which the central city may be only a part, an allocation of total county government expenditures between the central city and suburban areas must be made on some subjective basis. Even where the subjective basis is suspected of overstating expenditures in the central-city (e.g., population), such studies have produced evidence of significant fiscal disparities between cities and suburbs.[3]

The recent fiscal experience of central-city governments relative to their suburban counterparts is summarized in Table 2-1. These data show that per capita total expenditures rose at about the same rate inside and outside central cities in the 37 largest SMSA's, hence, the level of per capita expenditures remained higher inside cities. Relative to the growth in income, however, the increase in central-city expenditures was considerably higher, and as a result taxes per dollar of income earned increased markedly faster in central-city areas. By 1970, revenues raised from local sources per dollar of resident income were about one-third higher inside than outside central cities. This holds true even in the South, which on the average has higher per capita incomes in the central cities than outside. Even considering the greater tax potential for exporting, these disparities suggest a markedly higher tax burden inside central-city areas.

These data also lend support to the popular view (the municipal overburden view) that central cities (CC) are more heavily burdened by noneducational services than are their outside-central-city (OCC) counterparts. Over the

Table 2-1. Fiscal Disparities in the 37 Largest SMSA: 1970[a].

	Central-City (CC)	Outside-Central-City (OCC) Area	CC/OCC
Per capita expenditures			
1957	$213	$170	125%
1970	600	419	143
Average annual percent growth in per capita expenditures (1957–1970)	14.3%	14.4%	99%
Percent of expenditures financed from own sources			
1957	82%	68%	120%
1970	79	68	116
Per capita education expenditures			
1957	$ 61	$ 86	71%
1970	187	221	85
Per capita noneducational expenditures			
1957	$152	$ 84	181%
1970	413	198	209
Per capita revenues			
Local taxes	$289	$223	130%
State-federal aids	212	134	158
Locally raised revenues as a percent of income	8.9%	6.7%	132%
Locally raised revenues per dollar of state and federal aid received	$2.03	$1.70	119%

[a]All figures are averages weighted by population, unless otherwise noted.

SOURCE: Computed from Advisory Commission on Intergovernmental Relations, *City Financial Emergencies: The Intergovernmental Dimension* (Washington, D.C.: ACIR, Appendix B.

period 1957 to 1970, central cities, especially those in the Northeast and Midwest, have experienced a growing disparity with their suburban area governments and by 1970 were spending over twice as much on noneducational services. The opposite is true in the case of education expenditures where central cities still spend about 15 percent less on a per capita basis than do suburban governments. Moreover, they receive about 5 percent less in state aids per capita.[b],[4] One argument

---

[b]When calculated on a per pupil basis, expenditures are slightly higher in central cities, but state aids are slightly higher outside central cities.

for this disparity pattern in education vs noneducation expenditures is that, as a result of municipal overburden, the heavy drain on CC resources to service its resident and commuting population puts limits on the central city's ability to provide educational opportunities at a level equal to that in the OCC portions of the SMSA's. In this connection, it is interesting to note that in 1970, local school expenditures accounted for 51 percent of total expenditures by suburban governments in the 72 largest SMSA's, but only 29 percent in the central cities. Finally, only education *expenditure* disparities have been considered here, and education *service-level* disparities may be far greater, particularly if children from lower income families require special, more costly programs (for example, in terms of teaching approaches, class size and composition, and so on).

The conclusion one reaches from these data is that the metropolitan fiscal disparities problem is essentially that the tax burdens of central-city residents are, relative to suburbs, too high, and that education expenditures are not high enough.

Central-City Fiscal Problems

Apart from the issue of city/suburb disparities in service levels and tax burdens, there is a growing absolute gap between city government expenditure requirements and the ability of city governments to meet those requirements. On the expenditure side, the problems are familiar ones: an increasing concentration of the poor and the aged who presumably require more service than they can support, and the cost pressures induced by inflation[5] and public employee union successes. These pressures are compounded by the breadth of public functions performed by city governments—many cities simply do too much.

On the revenue side the income elasticity of the property tax is relatively low. Since most central cities are already built-up there is little property tax growth because of new construction (anyway, much nonresidential construction in central cities is in the tax exempt class), and major reassessments—never politically popular actions—are even less probable in a period when public services are being cut back. The use of local sales and earnings taxes has not resulted in a revenue yield adequate to meet the expenditure gap, apparently because the decentralization of jobs, residences, and retail activity has effectively limited the extent to which the city government can tap the taxable capacity of suburban residents.

In the face of this revenue/expenditure imbalance problem, the city's fiscal crisis has steadily worsened to a point where there are serious short-term cash flow problems facing city financial planners. In such cases, resort has been made to costly measures such as heavy short-term borrowing and the underfunding of retirement system programs.[6]

A final dimension of the city fiscal problem is that the distribution of tax burden is heavily regressive. The primary (and in some cases almost exclusive) reliance on property taxation results in a distribution of effective rates that is not proportionate to family income level. This suggests that poor central-city residents bear a relatively heavier proportion of total central city costs than do higher income families. It also implies that, e.g., an increase in police wages financed from local government property taxes, is effectively a transfer of real income from the lower to the middle income brackets within the city.

THE CONSEQUENCES OF FINANCIAL ASSUMPTION

On a basis of these dimensions of the urban fiscal problem, we argue in this research that any remedial measure must deal with three related issues:[7] (1) the supplementing of central-city budget resources either by adding new revenues or reducing expenditure responsibilities: (2) the reduction in central-city tax burdens relative to suburban tax burdens; and (3) the reduction in the relatively heavier tax burdens on the poor. It is against these three issues that the alternative of fiscal centralization—state and regional government financial assumption—is evaluated in this study. In this context, the purpose here is to present the *a priori* case for and against fiscal centralization. We do this in terms of a judgmental evaluation of the potential equity, efficiency, and cost implications of this reform alternative. The evaluation is limited in that we do not consider and compare in any detail the full range of reform alternatives. Instead, we concentrate on the ones proposed here—direct state or regional government financial assumption—and evaluate each against the present financing system.

Finally, it should be emphasized that our approach to studying the benefits of these reforms differs from that taken in the excellent Advisory Commission on Intergovernmental Relations (ACIR) series on the proper assignment of functions[8] in that we are concerned with spelling out the possible effects of particular changes, whereas their interest is with how functions may be best assigned between levels of governments. Hence, while the ACIR conclusions include guidelines for determining optimal actions, ours will only catalog the possible costs and benefits of state or regional government financial assumption.

Efficiency Effects

Two kinds of efficiency effects are relevant in studying the implications of the financing reforms proposed here: (1) *economic efficiency;* and (2) *technical efficiency.* Economic efficiency is a market concept, that is, in the private sector an individual allocates his income efficiently if he divides his consumption between every pair of goods such that the ratio of their marginal utilities to him is exactly equal to their price ratio. When all individuals reach this position, the outcome is called Pareto-Optimal; any reallocation will make at least one person worse off in terms of an efficiency or "welfare" loss.[10]

There is an economic efficiency analogy to the local public sector that involves defining maximum efficiency as occuring when *each* individual allocates his income between public and private goods according to his relative preference for public goods and the relative price of public goods. Hence, if there are no externalities the existence of a government always results in an efficiency loss, and the larger is the government and the more diverse are citizen preferences, the greater the loss.[11] Carried to its logical extreme, maximum efficiency in the no-externality case may be obtained where there is one local government for every different set of public/private preferences. However, in the more realistic case the benefits of public goods cannot be associated with particular segments of the population, externalities do exist, spill across jurisdictional lines, and are not perfectly reciprocal. In such a case, increasing the area and population served by any one government may improve the total welfare of society.

In terms of the popular arguments for government reform, economic efficiency gains/losses are usually referred to as the gains/losses from increased/ decreased local autonomy. Government functions such as police and fire protection, while characterized by major externalities, are obviously also characterized by neighborhood variations in how residents want these services packaged and the level at which they want them delivered. Measurement of these variations, however, is a problem that is far from being solved. So government reform on the basis of strengthened local autonomy is a difficult case to make.

Technical efficiency, on the other hand, refers to the relationship between government costs per person and the number of people within the government jurisdiction limits. The popular notion is that per resident costs decline with an increase in the number of residents covered by the government jurisdiction; hence, technical efficiency gains result because of economies of scale. Certainly there is much intuitive appeal to the scale economy argument. When one larger government replaces many smaller governments there are bound to be savings from the elimination of duplication of services, and with increased size may come a greater possibility for capital-labor substitution and consequent cost savings. On the other hand, many public functions are of the direct service type, characterized by high labor intensity, and it is difficult to see how increased size could induce any capital-labor substitution that would result in cost savings. And, of course, the antithesis of the elimination-of-service-duplication argument is the argument that larger governments will result in larger and more costly bureaucracies, leading one to conclude that decentralized service delivery is more productive. Finally, there is the possibility that there exist pecuniary diseconomies of scale, that is, that as government size rises so does public employee specialization and the strength of public employee unions, hence, wage rates are bid up to a higher level.

There is little agreement in the literature about the existence or nonexistence of scale economies in the provision of local public services. Since there is not a generally accepted proxy for public-sector output, the argument is not based, as it should be, on the underlying production function. Instead, most positive findings of scale economies are based on statistical results that show a negative relationship between population size and per capita expenditures. There are great statistical and theoretical problems with interpreting such results as showing scale economies, and about as many studies that find a negative relationship find a positive one.[12] If there is any consensus at all, it is that unit costs for the utility type services probably do decline as population rises.

Now consider the technical and economic efficiency effects of the creation of a regional financing district for city functions. The traditional argument would contend that as the number of residents of a jurisdiction is increased, there are technical efficiency *gains* and economic efficiency *losses*.[13] For example, in the case of the creation of a metropolitan government or a regional special district, there surely are welfare, or local autonomy, losses, and these losses are greater where the area population is more heterogeneous. On the other hand, the larger metropolitan government is more able to capture any scale economies that do exist. Whether such technical gains can be made depends on the services to be consolidated. In fact, those services where scale economies probably do exist—water, electricity, gas and sewage plants—have long ago been consolidated, and there is less reason to expect cost savings from the metropolitanization of the common municipal functions. In any case, cost reductions per se will almost never be observed when areawide or metropolitan government is created, rather, any scale economy benefits will most likely show up as improved areawide service levels.

From this reasoning one is tempted to conclude that movement to a metropolitan or regional government financing mechanism and delivery system will reduce local autonomy and cause economic efficiency losses, but will not likely result in large technical efficiency gains which show up as cost reductions. Hence, residents of central cities are probably better off in efficiency terms under the present system of fragmented government than they would be under regional government financing. The growing dichotomy of black cities and white suburbs reinforces this conclusion.

The alternative version of the shifting reform considered here—state financial assumption—is not likely to affect technical efficiency but may affect economic efficiency. For example, assume that full financial responsibility for the education function is transferred to the state government in such a way that the level of education services provided (financed) in any given local area is set at the statewide level. To the extent local preferences for education services differ from statewide preferences (as translated by the state legislature), there will be a local area welfare loss.[c] So state financial assumption is likely to lower the welfare of central-city residents, whose preferences for public services are likely to differ markedly from those of the average state residents.

The undesirable efficiency effects of state financial assumption might be reduced, or eliminated, to the extent local program control could be

---

[c]If, however, local education services generate a spillout effect—which the legislature can identify—a distortion in the level of local education services provided in any one community may be consistent with maximizing the level of state welfare.

maintained. Indeed, two major concerns voiced over the issue of relinquishing financial responsibility for education to the state government relate to economic efficiency. The first is whether adequate funding can be insured; the second is whether local decisionmakers will lose administrative control. Both amount to the worry that locals will get a package of education services after state assumption that is different from their present one, and one that they will like less.

There are clear reasons for suspecting that state assumption of education finance could result in a lower level of education spending. Since fiscal centralization would tend to promote equality of revenues (per student), it is possible that institutional arrangements may result in the underfinancing of education relative to other public services. For example, voters may feel more prone to reject a state school bond issue if in that year they are to receive no capital improvements in their district. Thus the relinquishing of local control over the level and composition of expenditures and the timing of capital expenditures may have a dampening effect on the overall level of education spending. However, this is clearly a long term effect. As is discussed in the cost section below, the short-run expectation is for equalization to result in cost increases, and thus relative overspending for education.

The second issue concerning local autonomy centers around how much freedom of administrative responsibility is retained by local officials after state assumption. Here there seem to be two divergent views. The first, held by the ACIR, is that once freed from the chore of selling local school bonds and tax rate increases, education policymakers can concentrate on the real issue of local control—the nature and quality of education. As a result, local decisionmakers and planners will have an even greater impact on the delivery of services than they now have. The opposing view is best characterized in the position taken by Coons, Clure and Sugarman,[14] who argue that no way has been devised to harmonize community control with equal opportunity of education provision, They see a tradeoff between state financing and local control. The results of state assumption, in such a case, are a distortion in the mix of education services provided, and therefore an efficiency loss.

Equity Effects

Regional or state government financial assumption may be offered as remedial action for two metropolitan equity problems: (1) tax burden and service benefit disparities between similar families in different jurisdictions (an interjurisdictional equity problem); and (2) tax burden and service benefit variations among families in different income classes (an interpersonal equity problem).[d] Though these equity dimensions are related—both are concerned with how real income is redistributed through the public budget—they are af-

---

[d]A third, and important, equity problem is that of variation in service levels and tax burdens among similar families in the same jurisdiction, i.e., a horizontal equity issue. For example, a renter may pay more property tax than his owner—occupier neighbor or a ghetto resident may have less access to public services than the high income condi-

fected in different ways by different reforms. For this reason we treat them separately below.

Interjurisdictional Equity. The stereotypical picture of the inequitable distribution of public sector activity in American metropolitan areas is one of poor central cities with low public service levels and high tax burdens, and wealthy suburbs where the reverse is the case.[15] The stereotype is very nearly true.

In evaluating the interjurisdictional equity effects of the two reforms suggested here, as against the present system of fragmented local government, we consider particularly the effects on city/suburb disparities in per capita education expenditures is implicit acceptance of the argument presented above—that because city governments are over-burdened by the substantial expenditure consequences of urbanization,[e] they are able to spend less than they desire on education even though their tax burdens appear to be higher.

The root of the metropolitan disparities problem is a fragmented government structure that separates the taxable resource base from expenditure needs. Clearly the creation of a regional financing district, in eliminating jurisdictional boundaries, is capable of eliminating service-level and tax burden disparities. Typically, when jurisdictions are amalgamated, wages, benefits, and workrules tend toward equality and whether service levels are equalized or not depends on whether, and how, service boundaries are redrawn. For example, in the case of consolidating fire services, there would ideally be a reassignment of firemen and equipment from suburban to central city areas, from richer to poorer central city areas and so on. In the education finance case, regional financing mechanisms have not been often posed as a potential solution to the jurisdictional equity problem[16] However, it is clear that regionwide financing districts can substantially affect interjurisdiction tax burden disparities. But, such schemes may result in local area residents paying more taxes in aggregate, since equalization of rates between city and county will lower city rates and reduce taxes on "exporting" industries. Depending on the relative concentration of such industries in the city and the county, and the tax used, the net effect of regional financing may include shifting burdens from residents outside the region to suburban residents.

State financial assumption also may equalize interjurisdictional disparities in education spending and tax burden. State governments can equalize

---

minium resident across town. Since this problem is not amenable to solution through government reform, it is not considered further here.

[e]There are three related arguments about why there is a municipal overburden. One is that suburban residents make costly use of core-city services and therefore impose a direct incremental cost on the city budget. The second is the indirect costs placed on the city by suburban governments when they effectively zone the poor out of the suburbs and therefore push higher service costs onto the city. The third is that because of the regional service-center function of the city, and in some cases because of its state dominance, it may have to provide a broader range of functions and subfunctions.

local spending levels directly and bypass the legislative process of reforming aid-distribution formulas. Moreover, there is an *a priori* reason to believe that state assumption will tend to eliminate local government expenditure variations—the establishing of statewide salary schedules, workrules, and performance standards. There is little strong evidence, however, that state assumption has in fact resulted in equalization for the social services, particularly education and health-hospital services within metropolitan areas.

In short, either of the reforms proposed here may in theory improve interjurisdictional equity, but the record is not clear in the case of regional financing schemes, and not good in the case of state financial assumption.

Interpersonal Equity. Because so little is known about the distribution of public expenditure benefits across income classes, analysis of the income distributional effects of the government reforms considered here is concentrated on the tax side. That is, in considering how state and regional government financial assumption affects interpersonal equity, we question only how resulting changes in tax structure might affect the tax burdens of families at various income levels.

The creation of a regional financing district does not always result in major tax structure changes. However, by moving financial reliance for some or all city services to an areawide property tax base, some amount of absolute property tax relief may be gained. An if the property tax is regressive, such a move may transfer some portion of financing responsibility from lower income city residents to higher income suburban residents. If the creation of a regional financing district were accompanied by a shift to reliance on a local income tax, then both interpersonal and interjurisdictional tax burden equalization would be stimulated to an even greater extent. But the Nashville, Miami, and Jacksonville experiences suggest that metropolitan governance will not always lead to a drastic change in the tax structure.

State financial assumption can have a marked and favorable interpersonal equity effect. The argument goes that any increment in financing from state tax sources is preferable on equity grounds to an increment from local sources, primarily because the major state revenue sources—sales and income taxes—are more progressive (or less regressive) than the local property tax.[17] Particularly if a state relies on the personal income tax, state financial assumption may result in a net reduction of tax payments by the urban poor.

Cost Effects

While the equity and efficiency effects of government reform have been given intensive theoretical and empirical treatment, the cost implications have been generally ignored in the literature. Policymakers, on the other hand, seem to be concerned most of all about cost effects. Somehow, they want to argue, financing and governance reforms will lower the costs of government. We attempt here to ferret out the reasons for expectations of higher or lower costs from either state or regional government financial assumption and to emphasize the difference between the long- and the short-run cost effects. We argue that in the short run, both reforms will tend to increase costs. In the long run the picture is less clear.

The two subsections below constitute a kind of differential cost analysis in that we assess the cost implications of each reform by comparison with the existing system of fragmented government. Our concept of the short run is not the economic definition, but simply a one- to two-year period, or a period long enough for the initial adjustments to the reform to be worked out.

State Financial Assumption. State financial assumption of urban responsibilities would have a number of effects on the level of and trend in total expenditures: (1) a shift to a more elastic and more flexible revenue base; (2) centralized control over the collective bargaining process; (3) shifting public program innovation from the local to the state level; and (4) a leveling-up of total local government expenditures resulting from the equalizing of input prices (primarily labor) and service levels. Only the latter is primarily a short-term effect.

Since state tax revenues (primarily sales and income taxes) are more income elastic than local property taxes, state financial assumption results in a greater overall growth in state/local government resources available. National estimates show the income elasticity of personal income taxes to be between 1.5 and 1.8, sales taxes between 0.9 and 1.5, and local property taxes to be between 0.7 and 1.1.[18] It would seem to follow that, *cet. par.,* a shift to heavier reliance on state revenue sources would result in a higher long-term expenditure growth rate.

There is further support for the argument that a shift to state resources results in a greater growth in resources available and, therefore, expenditures. There is more flexibility at the state than at the local level to make discretionary revenue changes, such as altering the tax structure or borrowing. This is because legal restrictions are less binding on state than on local governments and because local tax changes can be more closely identified with particular elected officials than can state-level changes. The latter implies more willingness to make unpopular tax decisions at the state than at the local level. As a result, increased reliance on state revenues should raise the long-term expenditure growth rate.

A final argument for an upward bias on expenditures because of the broader and more productive state revenue base is that a greater level of capital spending may result. States will be more willing to take on capital facilities construction and expansion because of the broader revenue base and because of their broader discretionary taxation and borrowing powers. Such capital expenditures have a multiplier effect on total expenditures because they require future maintenance costs, because they may occasion complementary type costs (for example, the construction of a new municipal stadium probably also requires changes in traffic control, streetlighting, streetwidening, bus routing, and the like), and because capital projects usually mean an interest cost in addition to the project costs.*f* While these are untested hypotheses, they seem plausible on a priori grounds as reasons for state financial assumption exerting an upward long-term pressure on expenditures.

Complete state financial assumption of a function would centralize the collective bargaining process. How this would affect the level of and the long-term growth in expenditures is mostly speculation, because research in the area is thin. On an intuitive basis, though, there are some reasons to expect *less* cost increment with centralized collective bargaining. State government generally has more of a research orientation than local government, and therefore may come to the bargaining table better equipped to assess (and perhaps resist) the long-term revenue implications of union demands. The less precarious cash position of state government (than their central-city governments) may result in less willingness to give up large benefit increments, for example, in anticipation of underfunding retirement system programs. Finally, there would seem more possibility for a state than a local government to set a program of public-sector wage/benefit increment guidelines.

In sum, the centralization of collective bargaining would seem to be a factor that could have a dampening effect, over the long run, on the level of expenditures.

One could argue effectively that shifting financing responsibility to the state level would reduce local area program innovation. The elimination of such "lighthouse effects" would have two implications: the loss of possible increments in public service levels, and lower costs. The latter occur because innovative programs usually have a high start-up cost, their continuation is typically costly, and they may fail completely or be cut out because of constraints. Finally, there is the leveling-up effect: in the very short run, state financial assumption will result in a total expenditure increase because of equalization of local expenditure disparities at a level near the highest of that presently existing. For example, if the state assumed complete responsibility for a function, it is unlikely that wages, pensions, performance levels, and the like, in various local government areas, would be allowed to remain disparate beyond estimated cost-of-living differentials. Moreover, it is likely that wage rates, pension benefits, workloads, and so on in the low districts would tend to rise toward that in the high districts. Wage-rate/benefit-level reductions in the high-paying districts would not occur, employment-level reductions in these districts would be

---

*f*However, for *any given level* of borrowing, state interest costs will tend to be lower because their bond ratings tend to be higher, particularly when compared to large central cities.

unlikely, and workload/service-performance reductions (such as student/teacher ratios, quality of fire department equipment, widening of service district boundaries) might take place. Together, these factors would result in at least a short-term increase in costs.[19]

The cost implications in the long run require analysis of whether, *cet. par.*, there is reason to expect an equalized system to result in greater or less expenditure growth than a more locally autonomous system where disparities are allowed. The positive answer might be drawn from a model that has the more progressive local units bidding for higher real wage rates, benefits, and service levels and carrying the less progressive units along. The negative answer might be drawn from a model where the increments gained under a locally autonomous system would have been greater.

Finally, to the extent state financial assumption results in the elimination of state grant programs, a dampening effect on long-term expenditure growth will be introduced. This effect is the result of losing the stimulative effects of state grants, which is the high-powered money feature of state aids. There is empirical evidence that such an effect exists, i.e., that on the average a one-dollar increase in state aid results in a more than one-dollar increase in expenditures.[20]

Regional Government Financing. Probably most difficult to evaluate in terms of long-term cost implications are intrametropolitan structural reforms such as the formation of regional service districts. Certainly in the short run, costs will rise because of a leveling-up effect.

The long-term cost implications, however, are unclear and remain essentially unresearched. The two most important questions to be answered about the costs of regional financing districts are (1) whether they increase the net flow of external assistance; and (2) whether they raise the level of services (and, therefore, expenditures) over the long run because of a quality effect.

Conclusions

From this discussion it should be clear that regional and state financial assumption is going to have to be justified on equity grounds. Efficiency and cost effects are simply unclear. Either state or regional government financial assumption implies an economic efficiency loss to city residents as they are less able to get the package of services they want. Whether there are technical efficiency gains to be had is not clear. Finally, the cost of government will *probably* rise in the long and short run under either scheme, implying, eventually, a higher tax burden for all residents affected by the reform.

The most relevant policy question for evaluating state or regional government financial assumption becomes clear: Are the jurisdictional and interpersonal equity gains great enough to offset the efficiency loss and long-term cost increases?

The conclusion that the reassignment of functions must be justified on equity grounds is not new; it has been the basis for numerous state assumption proposals. These proposals have, however, tended to base the equity argument on indirect evidence and even on impression rather than directly on the results of applied research. What appears to have happened is that well-informed persons have taken several related pieces of empirical analysis and created a plausable scenario for fiscal centralization. The view here is not that the scenario is wrong, but that the conclusions have not been drawn from appropriate hard research. The presentation of a set of hard results on the equity issue is meant to be the primary contribution of this research.

ALTERNATIVE FISCAL REFORMS

The regional government and state financial assumption reforms proposed here far from exhaust the list of suggested remedies to the urban fiscal problem. Indeed, over the past two decades the proposed reform measures have been almost as numerous as the panels commissioned to study these problems. Four general kinds of solutions, however, seem to have dominated: (1) reform of local tax systems; (2) government structure reforms such as the creation of metropolitan governments or regionally financed special districts; (3) reforms in the state and federal systems of grants-in-aid; and (4) the assumption of direct financing responsibility by state governments. This study is concerned directly with items 2 and 4. However, there is a relationship between these two and the tax and grant reform proposals in that state and regional financial assumption can result in accomplishing many of the goals sought under the alternative schemes.

In the case of reforms of local tax systems, it has been argued that one objective is to make the aggregate yield of the local tax system more income elastic. Proponents of this alternative argue that the property tax is inelastic with respect to income, and as a result cities are pushed to the limits of their discretionary taxing powers when faced with rapidly rising expenditures. So cities in one sense face a fiscal crisis due to definitions of legal taxable capacity and the inherent inelasticity of the property tax base.

Efforts to improve the overall elasticity of local tax systems have generally focused on improving the assessment process, instituting new taxes, or somehow taxing commuters through sales or earnings taxes. In general, however, these reforms ultimately depend on the natural growth in economic activity in the city area to raise the elasticity of the local tax system. State financial assumption would seem superior in that it bases the growth in available local resources on the growth in the state tax base, which—at least because of legal and geographic reasons—is considerably greater than the growth in the local tax base. It cannot be overemphasized that a major problem facing central cities is their declining economic base, a decline that is not likely to be soon arrested.

Efforts to improve the yield of local tax systems always are constrained by this decline.

Government restructuring alternatives, such as the creation of a metropolitan government, might also alleviate this problem of a low elasticity[g] by creating an areawide tax base. However, the underlying distributional effects of the property tax would remain if the regional government continued to rely on the property tax as a major source of revenues and if the property tax is as regressive as conventional wisdom suggests. On the other hand, if the creation of a regional financing district resulted in a shift to reliance on a local income tax, then restructuring would improve the overall income elasticity of the local tax system.

The other major reform alternative—adjustments in state aid systems—is also comparable to the state assumption alternative. One goal of state grant-in-aid policy has been to equalize expenditures and to relieve central-city tax burdens. As has been so clearly shown in the school financing literature, this has not been the result. While central cities do benefit slightly more on a per capita basis than do suburbs, the difference would not seem commensurate with the difference in needs. There seems little chance of major change in this pattern. The nature of state legislatures has changed from a rural to a suburban domination. So those who once advocated state aids as a means of redressing the central-city/outside-central-city disparities in education expenditures now favor state assumption.[21] In this sense the aid alternative has served to spur interest in the alternative of direct expenditure assumption.

NOTES

1. See, for various perspectives on the nature of the urban fiscal problem, William B. Neenan, *The Political Economy of Urban Areas* (Chicago: Markham Publishing Company, 1972); Dick Netzer, *Economics and the Urban Problems* (New York: Basic Books, 1970); Roy W. Bahl, *Metropolitan City Expenditures: A Comparative Analysis* (Lexington, Ky.: University of Kentucky Press, 1969); Alan Campbell and Seymour Sacks, *Metropolitan America: Fiscal Patterns and Government Systems* (New York: Free Press, 1967), Chapter 1; and Harvey Brazer, *City Expenditures in the United States,* Occasional Paper 66 (New York: National Bureau of Economic Research, 1959).
2. The thesis that local government employment is an appropriate proxy for local government output, and the implications of this thesis, are drawn out in Ronald Ehrenberg, "The Demand for State and Local Government Employees," American Economic Review (June 1973), pp. 366–379; and Roy Bahl and Richard Gustely "Wage

---

[g]If the property tax is more elastic for non-central-city governments, and there is some evidence that there is.

Rates, Employment Levels and State and Local Government Expenditures for Health and Education: An Analysis of Interstate Variations," in Selma J. Mushkin, ed., *State Aids for Human Services in a Federal System,* Part II of Services to People, State and National Urban Strategies, Public Services Laboratory, Georgetown University, May 1974). A detailed examination of the budgetary implications of public employment costs is contained in Richard Gustely, *Municipal Public Employment and Public Expenditure* (Lexington: Lexington Books, 1974).

3. Seymour Sacks has provided the research leadership in this field. See, for examples of the "fiscal disparities" literature which attempts to document these imbalances, the work of Sacks and John Callahan, presented in Appendix B in *City Financial Emergencies: The Intergovernmental Dimension,* The Advisory Commission on Intergovernmental Relations, (Washington, D.C., 1967) Vol. 2, Chapter 4. For attempts to explain these disparities, see A.K. Campbell and S. Sacks, op. cit.; and Woo Sik Kee, "Central City Expenditures and Metropolitan Areas," *National Tax Journal* 18 (December 1965): 337–353.

4. See Sacks and Callahan, *City Financial Emergencies,* op. cit.

5. There is some recent objective evidence that the expenditure effects of inflation substantially outweigh the revenue effects. See Robert Dinkelmeyer and David Greytak, "The Components of Change in New York City's Non-Labor Costs—Fiscal Year 1965–1970: Supplies, Materials, Equipment, and Contractual Services," Working Paper No. 13, Maxwell Research Project on the Public Finances of New York City (Syracuse, N.Y.: The Metropolitan Studies Program, Syracuse University, 1973); David Greytak et al. "The Effects of Inflation on Local Government Expenditures," *National Tax Journal* 27 (December 1974): 583–598; and David Greytak and Bernard Jump, *The Impact of Inflation on the Expenditures and Revenues of Six Local Governments, 1971–1979* (Syracuse, N.Y.: The Metropolitan Studies Program, Syracuse University, June 1975).

6. A useful analysis of the long-term budgetary effects of a retirement cost program may be found in Bernard Jump, "Financing Public Employee Retirement Programs in New York City: Trends Since 1965 and Projections to 1980," Occasional Paper No. 16, Metropolitan Studies Program, The Maxwell School, Syracuse University January 1975.

7. A discussion of these effects is also contained in Roy Bahl and Alan Campbell, "The Implications of Urban Government Reform: Efficiency, Equity, Cost, and Administration Dimensions," in *The Political Economy of Government Reform,* ed. Roy Bahl and Alan Campbell, (New York: Free Press, forthcoming).

8. We make no attempt at a major review of this literature. Comprehensive and well-integrated reviews are to be found in Robert Bish and Vincent Ostrom, Understanding Urban Government (Washington,

D.C.: American Enterprize Institute, 1973); and Advisory Commission on Intergovernmental Relations, *Government Functions and Processes: Local and Areawide,* Volume IV in *Substate Regionalism and the Federal System,* (Washingtin, D.C.: ACIR, 1974); and ACIR, *Performance of Urban Functions: Local and Areawide* (ibid., 1963).

9. ACIR, *Government Functions and Processes,* op. cit., particularly the first of these contains an excellent bibliography of related research.

10. A clear, nonmathematical treatment of consumer equilibrium and Pareto optimality conditions is given in Charles Ferguson and Charles Maurice, *Economic Analysis* (Homewood, Illinois: Richard D. Irwin, 1974).

11. This "decentralization" theorem is elaborated in Wallace E. Oates, *Fiscal Federalism* (New York: Harcourt-Brace-Javanovich, 1972), Chapter 2. Also see Robert Bish, *The Public Economy of Metropolitan Areas* (Chicago: Markham, 1971).

12. One of the more interesting of these statistical cost studies is Werner Hirsch's analysis of "horizontally and vertically integrated" urban public services. See "Cost Functions of an Urban Government Service: Refuse Collection," *Review of Economics and Statistics* (February 1965), pp. 87–92.

13. Formal treatments of this issue are contained in Michael Koleda, "A Public-Good Model of Governmental Consolidation," *Urban Studies* (June 1971), pp. 103–110; and Yorham Barzel, "Two Propositions on the Optimum Level of Producing Public Goods," *Public Choice* (Spring 1961), pp. 31–37.

14. John E. Coons, William H. Clure, and Stephen D. Sugarman, *Private Wealth and Public Education* (Cambridge, Mass.: Belknap Press of Harvard University Press, 1970), p. 202; see also Paul Cooper, "State Takeover of Education Financing," *National Tax Journal* 24 (Septemper 1971): 350.

15. A conceptual statement of interjurisdictional disparities as a part of the urban fiscal problem is elaborated in Roy W. Bahl, "Public Policy and the Urban Fiscal Problem: Piecemeal vs. Aggregate Solutions," *Land Economics* (February 1970): 41–50. An extensive study of intermetropolitan variations in disparities is continued in Alan K. Campbell and Seymour Sacks, *Metropolitan America: Fiscal Patterns and Governmental Systems* (New York: Free Press, 1967).

16. One example of such a plan, however, is the Louisville, Ky. schools, where a county wide earnings tax was installed to finance city and county schools. See Roy W. Bahl, "Louisville Intergovernmental Reforms for Fiscal Progress," *Fiscal Issues in the Future of Federalism,* Supplementary Paper No. 23 (New York: Committee for Economic Development, May 1968).

17. An interesting analysis of the progressivity of various state and local government taxes is Donald Phares, *State-Local Tax Equity: An Empirical*

Analysis of the Fifty States (Lexington, Mass.: D.C. Heath and Company, 1973).

18. ACIR, *State and Local Finances: Significant Features 1967 to 1970* (Washington, D.C.: ACIR, November 1969).

19. It is surprising that so little work has been done on this issue. See, for one example, Richard Gustely "Fiscal Equity, Efficiency and Governmental Consolodation" in *Evaluation of Two Tier Govt.: Case Studies of the Miami-Dade County Experience* Vol. II, R. Langendorf and R. Stefbold, editors, N.T.I.S., Springfield, Va., 1975.

20. See, for example, Seymour Sacks and Robert Harris, "The Determinants of State and Local Government Expenditures and Intergovernmental Flows of Funds," *National Tax Journal* (March 1964) pp. 75–85; Edward Gramlich, "The Effect of Federal Grants on State-Local Expenditures: A Review of the Econometric Literature," *1969 Proceedings of the Sixty-Second Annual Conference on Taxation* (Boston, Mass.: National Tax Association 1970); and Edward M. Gramlich and Harvey Galper, "State and Local Fiscal Behavior and Federal Grant Policy," *Brookings Papers on Economic Activity* 1: 1973), pp. 15–65.

21. The strongest organized constituency for state assumption would appear to be the ACIR. See their report, *Financing Schools and Property Tax Relief: A State Responsibility, A Commission Report,* (Washington, D.C.: ACIR, January 1973).

Chapter Three

Urban Observatory Cities: Economic Base and Fiscal Activity

The nine Urban Observatory (UO) cities are a representative cross-section of American central cities. Their economies range from diverse (Atlanta, Denver) to concentrated (Baltimore, Milwaukee), their fiscal problems from severe (Baltimore) to relatively slight (San Diego), and their populations from growing (Kansas City) to declining (Boston). On the other hand, they have several characteristics in common, the most important of which is a declining dominance with respect to their suburbs. Since the object of this research is to compare the equity and budgetary effects of state/regional government financial assumption in these nine cities, it would seem appropriate to begin with some detailing of similarities and differences in their underlying population and economic structures.

This chapter deals with a comparison of the socioeconomic makeup and employment composition, as well as with the fiscal-governance structure among these nine cities. Throughout, the focus is on how these characteristics somehow reinforce or weaken the case for centralization.

SOCIOECONOMIC STRUCTURE: AN OVERVIEW

The nine UO cities studied here—all metropolitan central cities—display wide variation in socioeconomic and demographic characteristics. For example, per capita income is one-third lower in Baltimore than in Denver; population density in the most crowded city (Boston) is nine times that of the least crowded (Kansas City, Missouri), and the proportion of the central-city population that is nonwhite ranges from 7 percent in San Diego to 51 percent in Baltimore. In spite of this wide variation there are three basic trends that most of the nine cities share: (1) each city is becoming a less dominant force in the SMSA, despite annexation; (2) city residents are poorer than their suburban counterparts; and (3) central cities are gaining increasing concentrations of population groups that may place relatively high expenditure demands on local governments while generating relatively few resources.

The data in Table 3-1 indicate that central-city populations grew at a much lower rate than did suburban populations, with extreme examples being Atlanta, Baltimore, and Denver.[a] Of the nine cities studied, only Kansas City, Kansas shows an increasing population share for the metropolitan area and this is largely due to annexations. There are two important implications of this declining population dominance of UO cities. First, the pattern is similar for all large cities in the United States, suggesting that the UO cities are representative of the nation's cities. Second, the declining population dominance of these metropolitan cities is generally reflective of the total relationship between the city and the SMSA, that is, city-suburb disparities in income and education have grown.

Two structural changes in city population appear common to the UO cities as well as to major U.S. cities in general: an increase in the percentage of the population that is nonwhite and in the percentage of the population over 65 years of age. The nonwhite proportion increased in all the UO cities—except Kansas City, Kansas—with particularly large increases in Atlanta and Baltimore. In general these central cities have received almost all of the growth of the SMSA's nonwhite population (not including Spanish-surnamed persons). For example, the central-city portion of the Milwaukee SMSA accounted for about 98 percent of the total SMSA growth in nonwhite population over the past decade. A similar pattern is observed with respect to the growth in the percentage of population over 65—all cities except Kansas City, Kansas experienced increases, with the largest increases observed for Atlanta, Baltimore, and San Diego. These trends have particularly important implications for this study, since increasing concentrations of the poor do suggest a growing revenue-expenditure mismatch, and heighten the concern about regressive local tax structures. Indeed, if the 1970s see an extension of trends such as presented here for the 1960s, some form of financial centralization would seem an almost essential intergovernmental reform.

The same picture of relative decline for central cities may be observed when the level and distribution of income is examined (see Table 3-1). These data show that the central city median income as a percent of SMSA median income declined over this ten-year period in all cities. The central cities became relatively poorer. Here, Denver is the extreme case, with Atlanta, Baltimore, Boston, and Milwaukee also showing large relative declines. This disparity in the relative levels of central-city and outside-central-city resident incomes may be underlined by comparison of the percentage of families with incomes below

---

[a]The small growth observed for the city of Atlanta occurred only because of annexations during this period. Without the annexations, Atlanta's central-city population would have declined.

Table 3-1. Selected Socioeconomic Characteristics of Urban Observatory Cities: 1960 and 1970.

City[a]	Annual Rate of Population Growth, 1960 to 1970		Central City Population as a Percent of SMSA Population		Population Per Square Mile	Percent of Non-white Population	
	CC	OCC	1960	1970	1970	1960	1970
Atlanta	0.2%	6.8%	47.9%	35.8%	3,779	38.3%	51.3%
Baltimore	-0.3	3.4	52.1	43.7	11,568	34.7	46.4
Boston	-0.8	1.4	26.9	23.3	13,936	9.1	16.3
Denver	0.4	6.4	53.1	41.9	5,406	6.1	9.1
Kansas City, Kansas[b]	3.3	2.4	11.2	13.4	2,961	23.1	20.4
Kansas City, Missouri	0.6	2.1	43.5	40.4	1,603	17.5	22.1
Milwaukee	-0.3	2.8	58.0	51.1	7,548	8.4	14.7
San Diego	2.0	4.4	57.8	51.3	2,199	6.0	7.6
Average[c]	0.2%	2.7%	48.7%	41.0%	6,125	17.9%	23.4%

[a]This Table excludes Metropolitan Nashville-Davidson because of the incomparability of the reported 1960 and 1970 census data.

[b]The relatively large population growth rates are for the most part a reflection of annexation.

[c]Unweighted.

Table 3-1. (continued)

City	Percent of Population Over 65		Central City Median Family Income as a Percent of SMSA Median Family Income		Median Family Income	Percent of Families With Incomes Under $3,000 (1970)	
	1960	1970	1960	1970	1970	CC	OCC
Atlanta	7.9%	9.2%	80.3%	71.4%	$6,275	18.0%	10.0%
Baltimore	9.0	10.5	87.7	78.3	6,796	20.0	7.0
Boston	12.3	12.8	77.0	67.7	5,921	19.0	5.0
Denver	10.8	11.4	105.7	82.4	6,920	18.0	10.0
Kansas City, Kansas	10.9	10.3	88.5	87.4	7,667	n/a	n/a
Kansas City, Missouri	10.8	11.8	87.5	85.2	7,474	20.0	10.0
Milwaukee	9.6	11.0	92.3	85.1	8,138	13.0	7.0
San Diego	7.6	8.8	94.6	94.4	6,223	17.0	14.0
Average	9.8%	10.7%	89.2%	81.4%	6,923	18.0%	9.0%

SOURCES: U.S. Bureau of the Census, *Census of Population and Housing: 1970*, series *PHC (2): General Demographic Trends for Metropolitan Areas*, 1960 to 1970; and Advisory Commission on Intergovernmental Relations, *City Government Financial Emergencies* (Washington, D.C.: ACIR, July 1973), A–42, Appendix B.

$3,000. In every city the central-city percentage is greater, and only in San Diego is the disparity not substantial.

In sum, the UO central cities are growing slowly, and their residents are becoming poorer in relation to their outside-central-city counterparts. Furthermore, the composition of the central-city population is changing dramatically, with growing concentrations of nonwhites, the aged, and the poor in general.

Another way to gain a general profile of the socioeconomic makeup of these core cities is to compare the industry of employment of its residents. As may be seen in Table 3-2, these cities are roughly comparable in terms of employment structure. The outliers in this comparison are Baltimore and Milwaukee which, to a much greater extent, rely on manufacturing employment. A more detailed breakdown of the structure of resident employment is presented in Appendix A, which shows location quotients for 41 three-digit SIC sectors.[b]

Employment structure differences have major effects on the extent to which state or regional financial assumption results in income redistribution. If a city's taxable property base includes large amounts of industrial property and these industries are exporting to a national market and if the property tax is shifted forward, local residents are paying a relatively smaller fraction of the local property tax. From these employment figures it would appear that, *ceteris paribus*, Milwaukee and Baltimore residents would gain relatively less in terms of tax relief if the local property tax were reduced by one dollar.

FISCAL STRUCTURE

It would be difficult, if at all possible, to develop a measure that would enable strict comparison of the magnitude of the fiscal problems facing the UO cities. However, a comparison of fiscal structures and trends, and of fiscal disparities, may give some indication of the nature of the fiscal difficulties facing these cities; and specific characteristics of individual cities may give some indication of the sources of such fiscal problems.

The wide variation in functional responsibility among the UO cities is a key to understanding the relative severity of their fiscal crisis. In general, the more functional responsibility a city has, the greater its potential resource-requirements imbalance and the more likely it is to benefit from financial centralization. These central cities, or their overlapping local governments, all have responsibility for education financing, while only Baltimore, Milwaukee, and Denver are responsible for welfare (see Table 3-3).[c] Apart from these two

---

[b]These location quotients are computed as the employment percent in any industry in a city as a ratio to the percent employed in that industry in the 76 largest SMSA central cities.

[c]Welfare is a county function in Wisconsin and, therefore, partially financed from city resident property tax payments.

Table 3-2. Percent Distribution of Employment, by Industry Sector.

	Atlanta	Baltimore	Boston	Denver	Kansas City, Missouri	Milwaukee	San Diego
Agriculture, Forestry, Fisheries and Mining	0.79%	0.47%	0.34%	1.84%	0.91%	0.51%	1.51%
Construction	5.72	5.19	4.40	5.11	5.22	3.61	5.03
Manufacturing	16.72	25.85	17.49	14.95	21.24	34.79	17.77
Transportation, Communication and Utilities	9.02	7.73	7.56	7.91	9.19	6.15	5.36
Wholesale and Retail Trade	22.03	18.54	19.39	23.02	22.77	20.74	21.08
Services	39.40	34.00	43.51	40.38	33.08	29.34	40.34
Public Administration	6.27	8.44	7.27	6.73	7.60	4.77	8.99

SOURCE: U.S. Bureau of the Census, *Census of Population: 1970, Detailed Characteristics, Final Report PC(1)-D1, United States Summary* (Washington, D.C.: U.S. Government Printing Office, 1973).

Table 3-3. Expenditure Structures and Trends: 1962 to 1970.

Expenditures	Baltimore	Boston	Atlanta	Denver	Milwaukee	Kansas City, Missouri	Kansas City, Kansas	San Diego
Per Capita Expenditure (1970)								
Education	$222[b]	$139	$218	$170[b]	$183	$169	$127	$186
Noneducation	417[b]	414	204	306[b]	218	245	117	137
Total	$639	$553	$442	$476	$401	$414	$244	$323
Common Functions[a] as a Percent of Noneducation Expenditure	42.4%[b]	39.2%	43.2%	35.5%[b]	58.2%	37.9%	61.0%	67.6%
Welfare Expenditures as a Percent of Noneducation Expenditures	22.9%	2.4%	—	18.9%	—	—	—	—
Education Expenditures as a Percent of Total Expenditures	34.7%	25.1%	49.3%	35.7%	45.6%	40.8%	52.0%	57.5%
Average Annual Percent Change in Per Capita Education Expenditure								
1962–67	10.5%	10.8%	19.0%	8.0%	10.7%	4.4%	9.7%	2.3%
1967–70	25.8	15.9	26.4	11.4	22.6	26.5	8.5	12.6
1962–70	15.1	12.3	21.2	9.0	14.2	11.0	7.9	5.4
Average Annual Percent Change in Per Capita Noneducation Expenditure								
1962–67	4.4%	12.3%	13.3%	17.2%	10.8%	13.7%	7.9%	4.6%
1967–70	22.2	0.1	18.8	12.8	6.0	21.4	4.9	4.6
1962–70	9.7	8.6	14.9	15.8	9.3	16.0	7.0	4.6

[a]Common functions include streets, police, fire, sanitation, parks and recreation, financial administration, general control and general public buildings.
[b]Includes welfare.
SOURCE: U.S. Bureau of the Census, *City Government Finances in 1970–71*, Series GF71-No 4 (Washington, D.C. U.S. Government Printing Office, 1972)

functions, the range of functional responsibilities of these cities varies widely as does the quantity and quality of services offered within the common functions.[d]

Three cities in particular—Baltimore, Boston, and San Diego—stand out in this comparison in terms of fiscal structure and trends. Some mention of these special circumstances may shed light on the nature of the urban fiscal crisis in general and its relationship to population characteristics and functional responsibility in particular. First, Baltimore stands out as having the highest level of per capita expenditures, primarily because it has the financial responsibility for the welfare function. Nearly 23 percent of city noneducation expenditures are for welfare, and, furthermore, the changing composition of Baltimore's population (see Table 3-1) indicates that continued responsibility for this function may induce an even more severe drain on the city budget. By comparison, while most other city expenditures on noneducational services slowed down, particularly during the 1967-1970 period, Baltimore's skyrocketed.

It is interesting to compare Baltimore's experience with that of Boston. In 1960 both cities were responsible for the welfare function. However, in 1969, Boston's welfare function was shifted to the state. As a result, Boston's growth in noneducation expenditures was almost zero over the 1967-1970 period, even though the change in the composition of Boston's population during this period was similar to Baltimore's experience. Thus it appears that removal of the responsibility for welfare finance from the city of Boston permitted a much less drastic increment in expenditures than would have resulted otherwise.

San Diego's fiscal structure and experience is also instructive. Of all the cities studied, San Diego showed the smallest central-city/outside-central-city disparities in socioeconomic characteristics. In fact, San Diego, in terms of income, population composition, population density, and so on, appears more suburban than urban by comparison with the other cities (see Table 3-1). The absence of a heavy concentration of the poor and the presence of a relatively strong resource base, together with financial responsibility for relatively few of the optional functions, leads to San Diego's relatively strong fiscal position. The city of San Diego is able to devote nearly 68 percent of its noneducational expenditures to the common city functions and still spend over 57 percent of its total resources on education.[e] In total, San Diego has the second lowest per capita total expenditures ($323) of the UO cities.

---

[d]All city governments have a set of functions in common—police, fire, sanitation, street maintenance, parks and recreation, financial administration, and general control—which are normally referred to as the common functions. The remainder of expenditures are usually referred to as the optional functions.

[e]The average proportion of education expenditures for the 72 largest metropolitan central cities is only 29 percent.

While the structure and trend of city fiscal activities gives some notion of the underlying sources of the urban fiscal problem, another dimension is the fiscal disparities issue—the disparities in expenditure levels and tax burdens that exist between city and suburban governments. To gain an overall picture of fiscal disparities in the UO SMSA's, expenditures by all central-city and outside-central-city overlapping jurisdictions are compared (see Table 3-4).*f* The results are quite similar to those obtained from comparisons of the 37 largest SMSA's.[1] In the UO SMSA's, noneducational expenditures in the central cities are up to three times as great as those in the outside-central-city portion of the SMSA. Again, Baltimore and San Diego set the two extremes. The disparities in education expenditures are mixed: three central cities show higher per capita expenditures than do the outside-central-city portions of the SMSA's. On the other hand, the cities of Boston, Kansas City, Milwaukee, and San Diego have relatively low per capita expenditures compared to their suburban counterparts. It would appear that one feature of the national disparities—higher noneducational and lower educational expenditures in central cities than their suburbs—is present in at least four of the UO cities.

In all of the cities studied, per capita locally raised taxes are higher in central cities than outside central cities, the ratio of per capita locally raised taxes in the central city to that outside the central city ranged between 2.06 in Atlanta and 1.04 in San Diego, with a mean ratio of 1.67. The ratio of locally raised taxes to income, which gives a crude measure of tax effort, shows a consistently higher effort by central-city than outside-central-city jurisdictions. In at least three SMSA's, the core city tax burden is over twice as high.

PUBLIC EMPLOYMENT CHARACTERISTICS

The pressures for increased levels of expenditure in these cities may also be examined in terms of relative increases in employment levels and in wage rates. It might be argued that while the former are apt to lead to real service-level increments, the latter may not—especially if wage rate and productivity increments are not related in the short run.

The data in Table 3-5 show that with the exception of Kansas City, all cities added at least one common function employee per 1,000 population over the 1965-1973 period. It is also interesting to note from this comparison that there is no apparent relationship between these increments and the 1965 employment levels. Wage rate increments were, in percentage terms, 2 to 3 times greater than employment-level increases. This result, be it a reflection of some catch-up phenomenon or not, indicates the very substantial impact of

---

*f*Comparison in terms of overlapping jurisdictions removes any distortions caused by intercity differences in functional repsonsibility.

Table 3-4. Per Capita Expenditures and Locally Raised Taxes for the Central-City and Outside-Central-City Portion of the SMSA: 1970[a]

| City[b] | Per Capita Expenditures | | | | | | | | | Locally Raised Taxes | | | | | |
| | Noneducation | | | Education | | | Total | | | Per Capita | | | As Percent of Income | | |
	CC	OCC	CC/OCC	CC	OCC	CC/OCC	CC	OCC	CC/OCC	CC	OCC	CC/OCC	CC	OCC	CC/OCC
Baltimore	$417	$134	$310	$222	$215	$103	$639	$349	$182	$221	$195	113%	8.0%	5.1%	157%
Boston	392	188	208	139	177	78	531	365	145	369	263	140	11.6	6.4	181
Atlanta	336	124	270	218	191	114	554	315	175	252	122	206	7.1	3.4	208
Kansas City, Missouri	316	153	206	169	194	87	485	347	140	253	157	161	7.5	3.9	192
Nashville-Davidson	210	57	368	168	115	146	378	172	219	163	62	262	5.5	2.7	203
Milwaukee	379	263	160	183	250	73	562	513	110	306	179	170	8.9	4.4	202
Denver	332	111	299	170	195	87	502	306	164	272	180	151	7.4	5.4	137
San Diego	298	245	121	186	227	81	484	472	102	206	198	104	5.7	5.9	97
8 UO SMSA's[c]	335	159	210	182	196	93	517	355	146	255	170	151	7.7	4.7	166
37 Largest SMSA's[c]	341	174	196	183	211	87	524	385	136	258	190	136	7.4	5.1	145

[a]These data include expenditures from all overlapping governments in the SMSA.

[b]Kansas City, Kansas is omitted from this table because it was not possible to present data by overlapping governments.

[c]Unweighted.

SOURCE: Computed from Advisory Commission on Intergovernmental Relations. *City Financial Emergencies: The Intergovernmental Dimension* (Washington, D.C.: ACIR, July 1973), Appendix B.

Table 3–5. City Government Employment and Wage Rate Levels, in Selected Cities

	Common Function Employment 10,000 Population			Average Monthly Earnings per Noneducation Employee		
	1965	*1973*	*Change*	*1965*	*1973*	*Percent Change*
Baltimore	120	145	25	$418	$693	66%
Boston	119	129	10	521	907	74
Atlanta	95	117	22	416	800	92
Kansas City, Mo.	79	84	5	461	838	82
Nashville	82	92	10	408	564	38
Milwaukee	72	99	17	689	1021	48
Denver	90	118	28	599	861	44
San Diego	45	55	10	855	1039	22

SOURCE: U.S. Department of Commerce, Bureau of the Census. *Local Government Employment in Selected Metropolitan Areas and Large Counties: 1965; 1973* (Washington, D.C.: Government Printing Office 1966; 1974)

public-sector unions on the expenditures of large cities. From this it follows that one important element to be considered in evaluating the financial centralization alternative is how it might impact this wage rate pressure on expenditures.

NOTES

1. As reported in Advisory Commission on Intergovernmental Relations, *Performance of Urban Functions: Local and Areawide* (Washington, D.C.: ACIR, September 1963), Appendix A.

Chapter Four

The Choice of Functions and the Leveling-up Problem

To insure that the policy implications of this study are realistic, each city was given considerable leeway in choosing the functions to be shifted and in assessing the total expenditure consequences of state/regional government assumption. In this chapter we outline the range of criteria used in selecting functions, present the range of functions chosen, and discuss the expected expenditure effects as among the nine cities.

CRITERIA USED

With respect to criteria underlying the choice of functions, the only guidelines offered were political reality, and that the functions should be selected after careful consideration of assignment criteria such as that suggested by the ACIR.[1]

1. The governmental jurisdiction responsible for providing any service should be large enough to enable the benefits from that service to be consumed primarily within the jurisdiction. Neither the benefits from the service nor the social costs of failing to provide it should spill-over into other jurisdictions.
2. The unit of government should be large enough to permit realization of economies of scale.
3. The unit of government administrating a function should have a geographic area of jurisdiction adequate for effective performance.
4. The unit of government should have the legal and administrative ability to perform services assigned to it.
5. Every unit of government should be responsible for a sufficient number of functions so that its governing processes involve a resolution of conflicting interests, with significant responsibility for balancing governmental needs and resources.

6. Performance of functions by units of government should remain controllable by and accessible to its residents.
7. Functions should be assigned to the level of government that maximizes the conditions and opportunities for active citizen participation and still permits adequate performance.

There is a voluminous literature on the subject of the optimal size of government to provide particular public services. Indeed, each of the seven points mentioned above has been subject to much empirical and theoretical research. As noted in Chapter 2, however, the conclusions as to the assignment of public functions between levels of government does not go much further than the general guidelines presented in the original 1963 ACIR study.

The choice of functions in these case studies was, in fact, in every case made on the basis of judgment about how these factors supported some functional shift that had already been given serious local consideration. The most common arguments were that the service had major spillover benefits to suburban residents, or the city's fiscal crisis demanded passing the financing of the function to a higher level of government. These two approaches to the choice of functions are well illustrated in the justifications offered in the Boston and Baltimore studies.

In the Boston case,[2] several criteria were used to identify local functions more suitable for state than local financing. The first is the efficiency of delivery of the service: for some functions—for example, solid waste disposal—technology makes it more costly per capita to provide the service separately through individual municipalities than to operate regionally based waste disposal facilities.

The second criterion is the degree to which residents of the service area are agreed as to the quantity or quality of the service to be provided. The greatest degree of consensus can always be found at the lowest jurisdictional level, but the Boston report argues that for the services selected for shifting, state financing will not result in service levels too different from any one municipality's preferences. For example, there is not likely to be much dispute among municipal officials as to correctional institution standards.

A third criterion is the identification of services that have significant spill-in or spill-out characteristics; that is, when municipally financed, they benefit or adversely affect residents of other local jurisdictions, which have no voice in their delivery, on the one hand, and on the other hand, services with these characteristics involve costs without commensurate benefits to the responsible jurisdiction and eventually generate taxpayer resistance that forces severe reductions in service levels. Vocational education and transportation are two good examples of this phenomenon.

The fourth criterion is that the area taxed to provide any service which affects a redistribution of services or cash (such as health and hospitals and veterans' assistance) should include enough persons in each group to make redistribution worthwhile. Underlying all of these concerns in the Boston case is the acute fiscal problem of the central city and its continued responsibility for a set of costly functions that the state government might be willing to assume.

The justifications offered in the Baltimore study are more directly related to the city's fiscal problems. Two sets of projections of a growing city government fiscal gap were made in an earlier Baltimore UO study:[3] the first based on the assumption of quality improvement in the level of public services; the second on the assumption of improvement in public service levels paralleling that of the 1965-70 period. Under the constant-quality assumption, Baltimore was projected to suffer a deficit in excess of $30 million, or roughly 20 percent of its property tax rate. The suburbs, on the other hand, were projected to suffer a deficit in excess of $100 million—an increase in property tax rates of two-thirds. The study concluded that without a substantial shift in state aid, a sizable differential in property tax rates and government service levels would arise in the near future. This result will hold even with increased federal revenue-sharing, for it does not significantly reduce the disparities between central city and suburbs. What makes these findings of particular importance here is the fact that all of the city's deficit under the constant-quality projection and 60 percent of it under the continuing-improvements projection is attributable to increased spending for schools. Hence, the city's fiscal crisis is closely tied to problems of school finance. On this basis, education is the only function considered in the Baltimore case study.

In general the UO cities might be split into two groups in terms of how they justify one or a package of functions for state or regional government financial assumption. One group considered certain efficiency/equity criteria but were essentially making the financial-emergency argument that the city budget must be relieved of some functional responsibility because of resource constraints. This group includes Baltimore, Kansas City, Milwaukee, and Boston. The other cities argued for the shift more in terms of equity/efficiency considerations. Two cities whose fiscal problems are presently not of emergency proportions—San Diego and Denver—also argued for shifting costly functions (education and welfare) on grounds that these will generate heavy future costs.

FUNCTIONS CHOSEN

The result of consideration of these guidelines, and of the political feasibility of various alternatives, is that a wide range of functions are considered candidates for shifting to higher levels of government. There was, however, considerable variation among cities, with some examining only one or two functions and others considering several expenditure functions or subfunctions. Predictably, the functions considered most often were those that lie at the heart of the fiscal problem of cities—education and welfare. The summary in Table 4-1 shows the

Table 4-1. Functions Considered for Financial Centralization[a] (S is state Government assumption; R is regional government assumption).

Function	Boston	Denver	Baltimore	Atlanta[a]	Kansas City	Milwaukee	San Diego	Nashville-Davidson
Education			S		S	S	S	S
Welfare		S				S		S
Transportation								
Mass Transit	S	R					R	
Airports							R	
Street Maintenance	S	R		R				
Public Safety								
Crime Lab							R	
Courts and Correction	S	R		R				S
Harbor Patrol	S							
Traffic Control	S							
Police Protection— general				R				
Arson Investigation	S							
Police Training	S							
Fire Protection				R				
Fire Boats	S							
Parks and Recreation								
Cultural Institutions		R					R	
Parks	S		S	R				
Libraries	S	R	S	R				
Stadiums							R	
Hospitals	S		S					S
Health Care	S		S	R				S
Sewage	S							
Planning				R				
Flood Control							R	
Solid Waste Disposal	S						R	
Veterans Assistance	S							
Vocational Education	S							
Air Pollution Control	S							
Business License Enforcement							R	
Elections								S

[a]The Atlanta study considered a number of subfunctions too detailed to note here.

functions considered by each city. The important implications of this list of functions is that there remains a belief that city governments still do more than they can afford to do, and consequently there remains a considerable need to change the balance of financial/functional responsibility among levels of government.

An important policy implication of these results is the perceived feasibility of shifting the financing of packages of subfunctions to other levels of government. Policy reform has too often failed to consider this option, and has focused almost exclusive concern on expenditure functions as though they were not separable. If a proper assignment of functions is to be forged out of the guidelines presented here, attention to detailed components of major classes of expenditure will be necessary. As will be shown below, the budgetary relief implied by reassigning the subfunctions is considerable—another factor often overlooked because of preoccupation with those functions that individually account for a major share of the government budget.[4]

COST IMPLICATIONS

As may be seen from the case study discussion in Chapter 6, the short-term cost effects of financial centralization are thought to be considerable. Based on subfunction-by-subfunction estimates of leveling-up effects, these case studies suggest increments ranging from 11 percent in Kansas City and 15 percent in Baltimore to nearly 30 percent in Boston.

It is likely that these leveling-up effects are underestimated. In almost every case the increment resulted from expansions of programs after centralization, and careful attention was not given to estimating the cost implications of equalizing wage rate and pension/fringe-benefit levels throughout the state or region.

NOTES

1. Advisory Commission on Intergovernmental Relations, *Performance of Urban Functions: Local and Areawide* (Washington, D.C.: ACIR, September 1963), and *Government Functions and Processes: Local and Areawide,* Vol. IV in *Substate Regionalism and the Federal System,* (Washington, D.C.: ACIR, 1974).
2. Katherine Bradbury, Philip Moss, and Joseph S. Slavet, *Reallocation of Selected Municipal Services to the State: A Municipal Finance Alternative* (Boston: Boston Urban Observatory, October 1973).
3. William Oakland, Eliyahu Borukhov, Frederick T. Sparrow, and Albert Teplin, *Baltimore Municipal Finance Study* (Baltimore: Baltimore Urban Observatory, July 1972).
4. A careful and interesting disection of a city budget into detailed subfunctions, for purposes of functional reassignment, is contained in Astrid

E. Merget, "The Expenditure Implications of Political Decentralization," Working Paper No. 3, Maxwell Research Project on the Public Finances of New York City, Metropolitan Studies Program, Syracuse University 1973.

Chapter Five

Tax Burden Estimates

The results obtained in this study depend heavily on the different distributional effects of local property taxes as compared with regional and state taxes. Accordingly, it would seem essential to pay particularly close attention to the tax incidence assumptions made in these studies, and to the data and procedures used in estimating the distribution of tax burden across income classes.

One key assumption was common to all studies. It was assumed that local property taxes would be reduced by the amount of expenditures shifted to the higher level of government. The only departure from this was the Baltimore study assumption that in addition to property tax reductions, the local piggyback income tax would be transferred to the state level to defray some of the increased costs of education assumption.

Three taxes were central in assumptions about how the regional or state government would raise the additional funds required: sales, income, and property (see Table 5-1). The only case in which a shift to state personal income

Table 5-1. Proposed Financing Devices.

City	Regional Government Tax	State Government Tax
Boston	—	Motor fuel, sales, and income
Kansas City	—	Sales, income, and residential property
San Diego	Property	Sales, income
Baltimore	—	Sales, income
Denver	Property, sales	Sales, income
Nashville	—	Sales, corporate income, and auto license fees
Milwaukee	—	Income
Atlanta	Income, payroll, sales and property	—

tax financing was not considered was Tennessee, where it was thought to be "not politically feasible."

The three steps necessary in carrying out this empirical tax burden analysis are (1) developing an appropriate and measurable income concept. (2) developing assumptions about tax incidence; and (3) estimating the burden distribution. A summary of the procedures used in these case studies, and a description of the resulting burden distributions, are the subjects of this chapter.

ECONOMIC INCOME

In this subsection,[a] the income distribution to be used in this study is defined, measured, and compared among the eight UO metropolitan areas.[1] Immediately below we suggest the definition of income that would seem most appropriate for tax burden estimates and compare this to the definitions under which existing data are compiled. Then we turn to a detailed presentation of a methodology for estimating an appropriate income distribution (which we refer to as economic income), and finally, we carry out the estimation for a number of metropolitan areas.[b]

The Income Concept
One long debated issue in tax burden studies has been the appropriateness of the income definitions used. The debate, for instance, between Musgrave and Tucker about the distribution of the U.S. tax burdens in 1948 centered around the choice of an income concept.[2] The difference in results obtained from using a narrow versus a broad defintion of income was enough to significantly effect the tax burden distribution. In order to obtain as good an estimate as possible of tax burden, it is essential to pay considerable attention to the income concept used.

The concept of income used in this study, as comprehensive a definition of income as could be developed for measurement purposes at the city level, is hereafter referred to as *economic income,* since it is more inclusive than either of the two basic concepts from which it is drawn—the Census definition and the Survey of Current Business definition.

The basic data used in constructing this estimate were obtained from the 1970 Census, the Office of Business Economics (OBE), and the Internal Revenue Service (IRS). Each of these data sources has characteristics that

---

[a]The reader not interested in the particulars of the income measure may skip this section without loss of continuity. Those interested in further detail are referred to Appendix B.

[b]The credit for developing this approach belongs mostly to Professor William Oakland of Ohio State University with the help of a committee including Larry Schroeder and David Sjoquist of Georgia State University, Kenneth Hubbell of the University of Missouri at Kansas City, and the authors.

facilitate the construction of an appropriate income definition, but each has severe shortcomings. The basic approach taken here is to adjust the Census data to account for the desireable inclusions found in the OBE and IRS income concepts. First, Census data are utilized because it is possible to derive from these data a distribution of income cross-classified by income level and family size at either the SMSA or central-city level of aggregation. The Census income concept, however, excludes capital gains and imputed rents, and is subject to substantial underreporting for non-wage and salary incomes. The OBE income estimate is used because it involves less underreporting of money income than does Census data, and because it includes certain nonmoney incomes not included in the Census data. OBE data, however, are not reported by income class. Finally, IRS data are used to estimate capital gains income, which is excluded from both of the other income definitions. A tabular comparison of these three income concepts is presented in Table 5-2.

The Census provides (by SMSA or central city) data for six basic classes of income, separately for families and unrelated individuals. These are (1) wages and salaries (*WS*); (2) nonfarm proprietorship (*NFP*); (3) farm proprietorship (*FP*); (4) Social Security (*SS*); (5) public assistance (*PA*); and (6) all others (*O*).[3] The Office of Business Economics provides data for four sources for both families and unrelated individuals combined. These classes are (1) wages and salary (*WS*); (2) proprietors income (*PR*); (3) property income (*PTY*); and (4) transfer payments (*TR*). These data are provided as a total for each source.[c,4]

To make comparisons between OBE and Census sources possible, the Census data are reaggregated as in the following manner:

1. Census wages and salaries were not altered because Census and OBE definitions are sufficiently similar. The only advantage of OBE data is that it is more fully reported.
2. Census and OBE definitions of proprietorship income are sufficiently similar to allow Census nonfarm proprietorship (*FP*) to be summed to OBE proprietory income (*PR*). Again, the advantage of the OBE data is fuller reporting.
3. Census Social Security (*SS*) and public assistance (*PA*) income were added. Further, it was determined that, for the United States as a whole, these two items represent approximately 71.08 percent of total transfer income. Therefore, the SMSA data was divided by 0.7108 to yield total SMSA transfer income (*TR*), or more concisely:

$$TR = \frac{(SS + PA)}{0.7180}$$

---

[c]Two minor adjustments were made to obtain the four sources noted above. The OBE amount for labor income was added to the category (1), wages and salaries, and the amount of personal contributions for social insurance were omitted.

Table 5-2. Comparison of Income Definition Used by the Census, Office of Business Economics, and Internal Revenue Service.

Jurisdiction Where Counted	IRS Residence[a]	OBE Place of Work[a]	CENSUS Place of Residence[b]
Source of Income:			
Wage and Salary	a. Wages and salaries	a. Wages and salaries	a. Wages and salaries
	b. Commission and tips	Commission and tips	b. Armed Forces Pay
	c. Piece rate and bonuses	c. Piece rate and bonuses	c. Commission and tips
	d. Payments in kind	d. Payments in kind	d. Piece rate pay and bonuses
	e. Reimbursed expenses— minus:	e. Other labor wages in- cluding:	
	1. Travel and transporta- tion	1. Private pension and welfare fund contri- butions	
	2. Education and other expen- ses connected with employ- ment	2. Pay of military reservist	
	3. Tax-exempt wage and salary earned abroad	3. Doctors fees	
		4. Jury and prison payments	
		5. Payments to prisoners of war	
		6. Marriage fees of Justices of the Peace	
Capital Gains	Included	Not Included	Not Included
Proprietors Income	a. Sole pro- prietorship and pro- fessional in- come that did not elect to be taxed as a corpora- tion	a. Money income and income in kind of sole proprietors, partnerships and coopera- tives	a. Money income from sole pro- prietorship and partnerships

[a]Income is counted in the period it is received.

[b]Income is counted in the period it is earned, i.e., when work is performed.

SOURCES: U.S. Department of Commerce, Bureau of the Census, *1970 Census Users Guide* (Washington, D.C.: U.S. Government Printing Office, 1970), pp. 108-109.

U.S. Department of Commerce, Bureau of Economic Analysis, *Survey of Current Business* (Washington, D.C.: U.S. Government Printing Office, May 1971).

U.S. Treasury Department, Internal Revenue Service, *State and Metropolitan Area Data for Individual Income Tax Returns,* No. 471 (12-64) (Washington, D.C.: U.S. Government Printing Office, 1964), pp. 10-14.

Table 5-2 (continued)

Jurisdiction Where Counted	IRS Residence[a]	OBE Place of Work[a]	CENSUS Place of Residence[b]
Source of Income			
Property Income	a. Rental income for rental of real property b. Excludes: 1. Dividends 2. Deductible expenses— i.e.,depreciation, obsolescence, depletion or net operating losses	a. Rental income of persons b. Imputed rents c. Royalties d. No capital gains or loss e. No deductions for depletion	a. Not included as a separate category, property income is a part of Census Component Incomes from other Sources
Income from Other Sources	Not an IRS Category	Not an OBE Category	a. Interest b. Dividends c. Property rentals d. Receipts for roomers and boarders e. Veterans pay f. Public or private pensions g. Periodic receipts from insurance policies or annuities h. Unemployment insurance and benefits and workman's compensation i. Net royalties j. Payments from estates and trust and alimony k.Net gambling gain 1. Nonservice scholarships and fellowship m.Money received from U.S. Manpower Development and Training Act. Excludes: 1. Lump sum receipts 2. Inheritance 3. Sale of property 4. Income in kind

(continued)

Table 5-2 (continued)

Jurisdiction Where Counted	IRS Residence[a]	OBE Place of Work[a]	CENSUS Place of Residence[b]
Income from Other Sources			
Transfer Payments	Not included in IRS data since basis for wage and salary etc. is work performed	a. Money income receipts of individuals from government and business for which no services are currently rendered b. Unemployment and old age provision of Social Security c. Federal civilian pensions d. Government life insurance benefit e. Federal military pensions f. Federal, state and local direct relief g. State and local pensions h. Cash sickness compensation i. Veterans aid and bonuses j. Government and corporate gifts to nonprofit institutions k. Individuals bad debts to business l. Business transfer payments to individuals	a. Cash receipts of Social Security pensions, survivors benefits, permanent disability benefits b. Public Assistance Income: 1. Aid to dependent children 2. Old age assistance 3. General assistance 4. Aid to blind 5. Aid to permanently and totally disabled. Medicare not included and payments received for hospital or other medical care excluded

4. So as to maintain the original total income for the six sources combined, the amount by which the original sum of Social Security plus public assistance was increased to become transfer income (*TR*), and was then subtracted from the Census category "other income." The decision is based on the observation that the Census reports a sizeable portion of transfer income

under the category other income (O). After removal of this Census transfer income from the category "other income," what is left is earned from property income. Therefore, the Census category O, after subtraction from Census transfer income, becomes similar to the OBE category property income (PTY), or more concisely:

$$PTY = O - \left[\frac{(SS + PA)}{0.7108} - (SS + PA) \right]$$

The major advantages of using the OBE concept of property income is that it includes the imputed value of owner-occupied housing, whereas Census property income data omit this form of nonmoney income.[d]

Finally, since neither the Census nor OBE data report capital gains as a part of income, IRS data on capital gains (CG) by SMSA are added as a fifth income source. In general, the effects of this procedure are to add the following to the Census income definition: (1) certain types of money incomes either not reported or underreported; and (2) the Census nonmoney incomes not reflected in the original Census data.

To summarize, three steps are required. First, it is observed that the Census categories "wages and salaries" and "nonfarm proprietorship" plus "farm proprietorship" usually are underreported when compared to their OBE counterparts, "wages and salaries" and "proprietor income." Thus, use of the OBE data as control totals for these two income sources tends to inflate Census data to correct for underreporting. Second, although this underreporting problem for the Census is also apparent in the collection of property income data, the major reason for using the OBE property income concept is to add nonmoney property income to Census income data, specifically, the imputed value of rents from owner-occupied housing. Third, the addition of IRS estimates of capital gains income data adds a source of money income not included in either the Census or OBE definitions. Thus, the income concept employed, called *economic income* in this report, is broader than the normal Census income definition in three major respects: the inclusion of certain nonmoney incomes, primarily the imputed value of owned-occupied housing; the upward adjustment of income under-reported by the Census; and the inclusion of capital gains.[e]

---

[d]The Census reports a considerable amount of transfer income in the category "all other" (O). The removal of Census transfer income from the category "all other (O) is described in Step 4.

[e]The choice of the term *economic income* is purely arbitrary, and not meant to imply that this definition includes all components of income.

Estimation of Economic Income

In order to derive a distribution of economic income, cross-classified by income class and family size, it is necessary to use a complicated estimation procedure. This estimation procedure is described in summary fashion here in terms of seven basic operations that are performed on the original Census data.

1. Census income data for the SMSA are aggregated from six components into four so as to conform with OBE data. These four categories are wages and salaries, proprietor's income, property income, and transfer payments. These are hereafter referred to as *source income.*

2. The total of the four source incomes for each SMSA is distributed among the fourteen income classes according to the national percent distribution for each source. After allocating source incomes in this fashion, the resulting mean family income for each income class is computed to determine whether it is consistent with the respective income-class boundaries. In general, it was found that it is not, i.e., many of the class means fall above or below the income-class boundaries.

3. In order to correct for this error, an iterative technique was devised to correct the distribution of source incomes. The purpose of this iterative technique is to correct the aggregate amount of income in each income class so that the computed mean (in any one income class) equals the national mean. The iterative procedure adjusts the value in each cell of the matrix so that the class mean equals the national mean but does so without changing the original values of each of the four source incomes.

4. Next, each of the four Census income totals is compared to its respective OBE source total to determine the degree of underreporting by the Census. This procedure shows the degree by which Census income data underreports income or omits nonmoney income. The distribution of income for each source is corrected so as to make the Census source total equal to the OBE source total for each source. For example, if the Census value for wages and salaries was found to be 0.9 of OBE wages and salaries, each of the values in the distribution of Census wage and salary income was multiplied by a factor of 1.1.

5. The above procedure corrects for underreporting of income; however, it does not correct for the omission of realized capital gains, which must be added separately. For each SMSA the total amount of realized long-term capital gains was obtained from Internal Revenue Service data, and was distributed among income classes according to the national distribution of capital gains income. With the completion of this step, there exists a 5-by-14 matrix of data. The five columns represent source income: (1) wages and salaries; (2) property income; (3) proprietorship income; (4) transfer income; and (5) capital gains. Each of the fourteen rows represent an income class. Summation down any one column yields the source total, i.e., wages and

salaries, and summation across any one row yields the aggregate income in that income class.

6. The next step in the procedure, the separation of the central-city income distribution from the balance of the SMSA, is done in the following manner: first, it is assumed that within any one income class, mean income is the same whether the family lives in the central city or the suburban portion of the SMSA. Once this assumption is made, the SMSA matrix can be divided into a central-city portion and an outside-central-city portion simply by apportioning the income in any one class according to the proportion of families residing in the central city. After completion of this step, there exist two 5-by-14 matrixes, one for the central city and one for the SMSA.

7. Steps 4 and 5, which corrected for the underreporting of income and omission of capital gains, results in the addition of so much income to each income class that the new means for each income class are, in almost all cases, above the original boundary of the income class. For example, in most cases the mean for the $1,000-1,999 class was approximately $1,500 before and over $2,300 after the completion of Steps 4 and 5. This implies that, had the Census reported income data more fully, then many of the people in the $1,000-1,999 income class would have been reported as having incomes $2,000-2,999 or $3,000-3,999. Similarly, the incomes of these persons should have been recorded as observations in the higher income class. To adjust for this improper distribution of families and incomes, a technique for the "bumping-up" of people and incomes was devised. Because this technique is complicated, and not easily summarized, the reader is referred to Appendix B for a complete description. In short, this bumping-up procedure redistributes people and incomes so as to correct for the incorrect assignment (by the Census) of families to income classes lower than the class in which they actually fell.

8. The final step in the income procedure is to distribute the aggregate amount of income in each income class according to family size. The family sizes range from one (unrelated individuals) to six or more. As in Step 7, the procedure for this step is complicated and the reader is referred to Appendix B for a complete description. In any case, the result is to provide separately for the SMSA and the central city, two 6-by-14 matrixes. The first matrix shows the aggregate amount of income cross-classified by family size and income class. The second matrix shows the number of families in each cell of the income matrix.

Comparison of Results

Utilization of this income-distribution methodology produces results that differ from the Census-estimated distribution of income in two ways. First, the broader definition naturally produces a higher overall level of income in each city; and second, there is a difference in the distribution of total income across income classes. These differences will drastically affect the tax burden distributions as compared to the results that would have been obtained using Census income data. Our argument is that economic income produces a better indicator of taxable capacity than does Census income, and hence will result in a better tax burden estimate.

The broader definition—economic income—produces a level of income that is from one-fifth to one-third higher than the Census definition, and raises average income for the ten cities studied from $9,486 to $12,327 (see Table 5-3).

The second difference is a change in the distribution of income. This effect is less easily described. To summarize the distribution effect, two summary measures are presented: Gini coefficients and the percent of family units with incomes less than 75 percent of mean family income. Combining these measures we conclude that the distribution of income tends to be more equitable than is indicated by the Census data, though the difference is very slight.

INCIDENCE ASSUMPTIONS

Property Taxes

There is currently much disagreement in the tax incidence literature about who bears the property tax. The issue centers on whether the tax is an excise tax, in which case the residential portion is borne by occupiers and the nonresidential portion by consumers, or a profits-type tax, in which case it is borne by owners of capital. Since this research is, in large, about the incidence implications of property tax reductions, the issue is of paramount importance here.

The implications of these two views for tax equity are diametrically opposite. If the conventional position of forward shifting is valid, the incidence of the property tax will be regressive, owing to the fact that housing expenditures in particular, and consumption expenditures in general, do not increase proportionately with income.[f,5] If capital owners bear the burden of the property tax (the new view), incidence will be progressive, since it is well documented that capital income accrues disproportionately to upper income classes.[6]

With the sole exception of the Milwaukee analysis, the conventional view was held in these case studies: the residential property tax was assumed to fall on consumers of housing. The nonresidential property tax was assumed to fall on consumption in general, partly on local residents and partly exported to consumers outside the region.

---

[f]Even here there is debate about whether or not housing expenditures increase more than proportionally with income. This controversy, however, centers around whether or not the income concept is appropriate. Our economic income concept is clearly more inclusive than that used in past studies, though it still is an annual rather than a permanent measure.

Table 5-3. Comparison of Economic and Census Income, by City.

	Atlanta	Baltimore	Boston	Denver	Kansas City, Kansas	Kansas City, Missouri	Milwaukee	Nashville-Davidson	San Diego	New York City
Aggregate Income										
Census Income (thousands)	$1,564,177	$2,602,768	$1,873,462	$1,824,481	$480,706	$1,663,289	$2,290,855	$1,381,875	$2,432,178	$31,233,429
Economic Income (thousands)	2,030,034	3,344,176	2,562,023	2,286,605	596,476	2,217,835	3,034,306	1,827,691	2,938,757	40,711,721
Percent Difference	29.8%	28.5%	36.8%	25.3%	24.1%	31.8%	32.5%	32.3%	20.8%	30.7%
Difference in Income Distribution										
Census Income Gini Coefficient	0.572	0.436	0.469	0.448	0.368	0.424	0.394	0.442	0.477	0.441
Economic Income Gini Coefficient	0.466	0.422	0.443	0.431	0.367	0.397	0.378	0.438	0.477	0.436
Difference in Gini Coefficient	-0.106	-0.014	-0.026	-0.017	-0.001	-0.027	-0.016	-0.004	0.000	0.005
Difference in Average Family Income										
Mean Census Income per Family Unit	$8,309	$8,084	$6,959	$8,869	$8,294	$8,927	$8,760	$8,995	$8,204	$10,253
Percent of Family Units 75 Percent of the Mean or Less	55.0%	51.3%	50.5%	51.5%	44.2%	48.3%	43.1%	48.8%	53.9%	53.0%
Mean Economic Income per Family Unit	$10,784	$10,388	$9,516	$10,864	$10,292	$11,762	$11,603	$11,898	$9,913	$13,365
Percent of Family Units 75 Percent of Mean or Less	49.9%	46.9%	43.5%	47.9%	41.6%	45.9%	43.0%	48.3%	53.8%	50.7%

In the Milwaukee study, the land portion residential property tax was assumed to be borne by families in proportion to their property income, the improvements portion by consumers of housing and the nonresidential property tax by consumers in general.

Non-Property Taxes

Personal income taxes were assumed to be borne by income recipients. The corporate income tax, included in the Nashville study, is assumed to be fully shifted forward and therefore partly exported. In the case of the regional payroll tax, proposed in the Atlanta study, it is assumed to be borne by the wage earners with no shifting taking place. All sales and license taxes are assumed to be borne by payers. Adjustment is made in all cases for exporting.

TAX BURDEN ESTIMATION

Similar procedures were followed by all UO cities in allocating tax burdens among income classes. The detail and care taken to account for the specifics that affect tax burden variations vary widely among these studies, and each warrants careful examination.[7] Only a cursory summary of procedures and results are presented here.

In the case of the residential property tax, an average housing value in each economic income class, cross-classified by family size, was estimated from fourth-count *Census of Population* data, from various consumer expenditure surveys, and from local data.[g] From these data on housing value/rental equivalents, total property tax payments were estimated by one of two methods: (1) the calculation of a representative property tax bill: or (2) the allocation of total tax liability across income classes according to the share of total taxable housing value.[h] In either case, care was taken to incorporate local property tax provisions in adjusting estimated housing value to conform to the taxable property tax base.

In the case of nonresidential property taxes, local data were used to estimate the "exported" share. The remainder, assumed to affect prices paid by local residents, is allocated across income classes according to total consumption.

Sales taxes were estimated for family sizes and income classes by using the optional sales tax tables provided by the IRS on the federal income tax forms.

---

[g]Two general approaches were taken. Under the first, Census tract data were used to estimate the housing value/income relationship, usually with a simple linear regression. Under the second, survey research results were used to impute a housing value equivalent to each income class.

[h]When the former procedure was chosen, then it was usually necessary to "force" the total payments to add to an appropriate control total. This procedure involves adding or subtracting some amount from the representative tax bill.

Income taxes were allocated according to taxable income in each income class. Taxable income was estimated by adjusting the comprehensive economic income definition to particular state/local taxable income definitions.

Motor fuel taxes were allocated among Boston residents according to personal income, and auto license fees among Nashville residents according to automobile ownership by income class.

There are marked variations among the cities in the specific data used and in the exact allocation procedures. While these refinements are in some cases methodological additions to the empirical tax incidence literature, and while they may affect the results obtained here, their presentation would require more space than is available here. The reader is referred to the individual case studies presented in Chapter 6.

TAX BURDEN RESULTS

The difference among these cities in the distribution of effective rates across income classes is a function of several factors: incidence assumptions, estimation procedures, data choices, the composition of the tax structure, and the equity features of particular state and local taxes. Hopefully the standardized approach taken here will permit abstracting from the first three of these effects.

The distribution of property tax burdens on central-city residents, as estimated in each of the case studies, is presented in Table 5-4. These results show a wide variation among cities in the level and regressivity of the local property tax. Boston stands out as having a relatively heavier property tax burden at all levels of income, and Atlanta as having a particularly low effective property tax rate. In terms of regressivity in effective rates, Boston and Baltimore show particularly regressive structures.

In order to assess the potential impact of reassignment on the tax burdens of the city poor, it is necessary to compare the property tax burden with the overall burden for all taxes involved. These results, presented in Table 5-5, show that the overall burden in every case is regressive.[i]

NOTES

1. For more detail, see the Appendixes in Larry Schroeder, David Sjoquist, and William Wilken, *Shifting Public Service Functions: Expenditure-Revenue Effects and Political Feasibility* (Atlanta: Atlanta Urban Observatory, April 1974).

[i]The reader is cautioned about interpreting the results for the under-$1,000 income class. The problem results from the difficulty of identifying families/unrelated individuals with economic incomes that low. The important point is that it clearly does not include the aged poor or those on relief, since transfer payments received would push them above the $1,000 boundary.

Table 5-4.   Central-City Residential Property Tax Burdens, by Income Class (in cents per dollar of income).

Economic Income Class	Atlanta	Baltimore	Nashville	San Diego	Denver	Kansas City, Kansas	Kansas City, Missouri	Boston[a]
$0 - 999	1.12¢	8.26¢	n.c.	37.50¢	2.75¢	24.26¢	32.50¢	n.c.
1,000 - 1,999	0.42	8.26	n.c.	11.70	2.75	4.65	8.43	18.10¢
2,000 - 2,999	0.36	8.26	n.c.	6.73	2.75	3.89	5.89	11.00
3,000 - 3,999	0.49	2.64	3.11	5.92	2.75	3.23	4.46	7.51
4,000 - 4,999	0.59	2.64	2.37	6.24	2.51	3.39	3.51	5.64
5,000 - 5,999	0.64	2.40	2.03	4.84	2.51	3.51	3.31	5.11
6,000 - 6,999	0.67	2.40	1.74	4.42	2.51	3.18	3.17	4.46
7,000 - 7,999	0.61	2.29	1.54	3.69	2.58	2.93	3.09	4.08
8,000 - 8,999	0.61	2.29	1.43	3.66	3.07	2.71	3.01	3.76
9,000 - 9,999	0.58	2.29	1.38	3.76	3.07	2.51	2.91	3.62
10,000 - 11,999	0.61	2.11	1.35	3.18	4.51	2.42	2.75	3.21
12,000 - 14,999	0.43	2.11	1.18	2.82	4.90	2.42	3.05	2.94
15,000 - 24,999	0.39	1.94	1.10	2.40	4.69	2.80	3.08	4.98
25,000 and over	0.42	1.55	0.75	1.83	2.64	2.04	1.96	2.16

[a]Effective rates estimated at class midpoint; $25,000 used as midpoint for top class.

Table 5-5. Burden of Selected State-Local Taxes on Central-City Residents (in cents per dollar of income).

Economic Income Class	Baltimore	Nashville[a]	San Diego[b]	Kansas City, Kansas[c]	Kansas City, Missouri[c]	Boston[d]
$0 - 999	12.91¢	20.11¢	20.80¢	24.26¢	21.31¢	n.c.
1,000 - 1,999	12.91	20.11	11.85	5.88	6.58	19.82¢
2,000 - 2,999	12.91	20.11	9.34	5.06	5.06	14.75
3,000 - 3,999	6.06	16.51	8.00	4.48	4.21	10.98
4,000 - 4,999	6.06	14.30	6.52	4.49	3.49	8.91
5,000 - 5,999	6.18	13.13	6.74	4.66	3.53	9.17
6,000 - 6,999	6.18	11.97	6.42	4.37	3.40	9.11
7,000 - 7,999	7.12	11.65	6.21	4.10	3.47	10.02
8,000 - 8,999	7.12	10.66	6.46	3.93	3.48	9.82
9,000 - 9,999	7.12	10.21	6.23	3.78	3.48	9.74
10,000 - 11,999	7.56	9.56	6.17	4.07	3.49	9.25
12,000 - 14,999	7.56	8.62	6.17	4.12	3.82	9.14
15,000 - 24,999	7.74	7.53	6.03	4.89	3.92	8.84
25,000 and over	8.72	5.30	5.50	2.62	2.77	8.45

[a]Includes property, sales, liquor, tobacco, corporate and personal income, auto license and gasoline taxes.
[b]Includes property, income, and sales taxes.
[c]Includes real estate, property, sales, income and earnings.
[d]Includes property, income, sales and motor fuel excise taxes.

2. See R. A. Musgrave et al., "The Distribution of Tax Payments by Income Groups: A Case Study for 1948," *National Tax Journal* (March 1951), pp. 6-53; and Rufus Tucker, "Distribution of Tax Burdens in 1948," *National Tax Journal* 4 (September 1971): 270.
3. These data are available from U.S. Department of Commerce, Bureau of Census, Census, Fourth Count, *General Social and Economic Characteristics* (Washington, D.C.: Government Printing Office, 1970), Table 89.
4. U.S. Department of Commerce, Office of Business Economics, *Survey of Current Business*, (Washington, D.C.: Government Printing Office, May 1971) p. 21.
5. See Henry Aaron, *Shelters and Subsidies: Who Benefits from Federal Housing Policies?* (Washington, D.C.: Brookings, 1972).
6. For a demonstration of the distributional implications of the "new view" and "traditional view" assumptions, see Joseph Pechman and Benjamin Okner, *Who Bears the Tax Burden?* (Washington, D.C.: Brookings, 1974); and Henry J. Aaron, *Who Pays the Property Tax? A New View* (Washington, D.C.: Brookings, 1975).
7. Particularly thorough presentations of the estimation procedures are contained in William Oakland and Eliyahu Borukhov, *Incidence and Other Fiscal Impacts of the Reform of Educational Finance: A Case Study of Baltimore* (Baltimore: Baltimore Urban Observatory, April 1974); Larry D. Schroeder, David L. Sjoquist, and William Wilkens, *Spending and Tax Effects of Expanding Local Government Services Districts* (Atlanta: Atlanta Urban Observatory, March 1973); and K. Hubbell, J. Olson, S. Ramenossky and J. Ward, *Alternative Methods for Financing Public Services: The Cases of Education and Welfare, Kansas City, Missouri* (Kansas City, Mo.: Kansas City Urban Observatory, August 1973).

Chapter Six

Individual Case Study Results

The results of careful case-study analyses reveal that state financial assumption would probably have positive effects on the distribution of income by lowering the overall regressivity of the state/local tax system. However, these results also suggest that overall service costs will rise in the event of fiscal centralization. These findings hold in every study. However, these results are not so uniform with respect to a number of other possible effects of state financial assumption, specifically, about how centralization affects: (1) the budgetary position of the central city; (2) the *level* of central-city resident tax burdens; and (3) inter-jurisdictional fiscal disparities.

It is not possible to summarize completely these case studies here—each is a substantial volume in itself. Rather, the intent is to present the basic findings of each case study and to summarize its position about the feasibility and the costs and benefits of the state assumption alternative. Details of the methodology used in each case study are not presented.

THE MODEL

To understand the model used to generate the estimated tax burden effects of fiscal centralization in summary form, consider, as an example, the effects of shifting education expenditures. Let education expenditures from own sources in the state be the sum of that made by the central city (E_1) and that made by all other local governments (E_2). Assume that the city, other local governments, and the state export—to residents of other states—tax percentages $(1 - \alpha_1)$, $(1 - \alpha_2)$, and $(1 - \alpha_3)$ respectively; that is, the burden of expenditures on city residents is $\alpha_1 E_1$. If the state assumes direct financial responsibility with no leveling-up, state expenditures rise by $E_1 + E_2$, and state resident tax liability by $\alpha_3(E_1 + E_2)$. Now if the state tax burden is distributed between the central city and all other local governments in proportions γ_1,

γ_2, then the aggregate change in central-city resident tax liability (dT_1) may be written as:

$$dT_1 = \gamma_1 \alpha_3 (E_1 + E_2) - \alpha_1 E_1 \qquad (6\text{-}1)$$

Hence, central-city residents in aggregate will experience tax relief so long as

$$\gamma_1 < (\frac{\alpha_1}{\alpha_3}) \frac{E_1}{E_1 + E_2} \qquad (6\text{-}2)$$

The tax burden change for a family in the ith income class in the central city (dT_{1i}) may be written

$$dT_{1i} = S_i [\gamma_1 \alpha_3 (E_1 + E_2)] - \beta_i (\alpha_1 E_1) \qquad (6\text{-}3)$$

where

β_i = the share of central-city taxes paid by a family in the ith income class
S_i = the share of any given amount of state taxes paid by a family in the ith income class

If leveling-up of amount K is allowed, Equations (6-1) through (6-3) become

$$dT_1 = \gamma_1 \alpha_3 (E_1 + E_2 + K) - \alpha_1 E_1 \qquad (1a)$$

$$\gamma_1 < (\frac{\alpha_1}{\alpha_3}) (\frac{E_1}{E_1 + E_2 + K}) \qquad (2a)$$

$$dT = S_i [\gamma_1 \alpha_3 (E_1 + E_2 + K)] - \beta_i (\alpha_1 E_1) \qquad (3a)$$

Three main implications may be drawn from these equations: (1) the increase in tax liability to the city will be greater to the extent leveling-up occurs; (2) the tax liability on the central city will be greater to the extent its share of state tax payments exceeds its share of expenditures on the shifted function; (3) the net increase in tax liability to city residents will be less to the extent the state government is able to export a greater share of its taxes than is the city government.

BOSTON[1]

It has been argued that the chronic crisis in municipal finance in Massachusetts is an overworked property tax.[2] By 1972, property taxes per capita in Boston had reached $345, about 3.5 times the national average. This overdependence on the property tax was attributed to both failure to reallocate traditional patterns of functional responsibility between local and state governments, and failure to shift the financing of certain costly services—health and hospitals, veterans benefits, courts, corrections, mass transit, regional parks, regional sewage treatment, and the like—away from local property taxes to broader-based and more elastic statewide sources of revenue.

Largely for these reasons the Boston report recommends that the administration and financing of a selected group of public services be shifted from municipalities to the Massachusetts state government.

Using mostly economic efficiency guidelines, the Boston UO study identified as candidates for shifting the group of eleven functions and subfunctions. Since no single function accounts for more than a small percentage of the 1970 budget, we evaluate here the effect on city taxpayers of shifting all eleven as a package. This package in total represents approximately 27 percent of city government expenditures from "own resources," or about $115 per capita at 1970 levels. The data in Table 6-1 describe the 1970 level of expenditures on the functions shifted, and indicate the percent of locally raised revenues accounted for by each major expenditure class. Hence $236 million is the amount to be raised by the state government in 1970 in the no-leveling-up case. The Boston study includes evaluation of both the no-leveling-up case, for 1970, and the leveling-up case, where expenditure increments are estimated for 1973.

Specifically, the total impact of the shift of services on affected governmental jurisdictions when leveling-up is allowed may be capsuled as follows (see Table 6-2): the total estimated savings to the city of Boston of the proposed shifts in 1973 would have been about $90 million. The estimated savings to all other municipalities in 1973 would total about $190 million. With the anticipated changes in service levels once the state assumes the administration and/or financing of the services, the Commonwealth's total obligation will increase by an estimated $363 million.

It is assumed that Boston and other municipalities would experience property tax reductions equivalent to existing levels of expenditures on the shifted functions.[a] Two alternatives were explored for financing the additional

---

[a]It is estimated that Boston's property tax reduction would be equivalent to about 26 percent of the 1973 property tax levy; tax reductions to all other municipalities would amount to about 11 percent of their aggregate 1973 property tax levy.

Table 6-1. Expenditures for Boston Municipal Services Recommended for Shifting to State: 1970.

Function and Service	City of Boston	All Municipalities Excluding Boston	All Municipalities
Public Safety			
Police traffic enforcement	$2,500,000	$4,800,000	$ 7,300,000
Harbor patrol	213,000	–	213,000
Crime laboratory	83,000	–	83,000
Police training	286,000	292,000	578,000
Arson investigation	146,000	–	146,000
Fire boats	476,000	–	476,000
Subtotal	$ 3,704,000(1.4%)[a]	$ 5,092,000	$ 8,796,000
Transportation			
Street maintenance and related street services	$ 3,757,000	$12,096,000	$15,853,000
Public transit	24,940,000	26,705,000	51,645,000
Subtotal	$28,697,000(105%)[a]	$38,801,000	$67,498,000
Waste Disposal			
Solid waste	$ 2,051,000	$18,857,000	$20,908,000
Sewage	4,414,000	11,831,000	16,245,000
Subtotal	$ 6,465,000(2.4%)[a]	$30,688,000	$37,153,000
County Courts and Corrections			
Courts	$ 7,515,000	$23,051,000	$30,566,000
Corrections	3,086,000	6,811,000	9,897,000
Subtotal	$10,601,000(3.9%)[a]	$29,862,000	$40,463,000
Veterans Assistance	$ 3,637,000(1.3%)[a]	$12,852,000	$16,489,000
Health and Hospitals			
Municipal health and hospital services	$11,869,000	$15,101,000	$26,970,000
School health services	821,000	3,889,000	4,710,000
County hospital assessments	–	3,854,000	3,854,000
Subtotal	$12,690,000(4.7%)[a]	$22,844,000	$35,534,000
Regional Parks and Recreation	$ 4,155,000(1.5%)[a]	$13,654,000	$17,807,000
Vocational Education	$ 1,594,000(0.6%)[a]	$ 8,886,000	$10,480,000
Regional Library Services	$ 2,200,000(0.8%)[a]	–	$ 2,200,000
Air Pollution Control			
City air pollution control	$ 57,000	–	$ 57,000[b]
Regional assessments	29,000	$ 178,000	207,000
Subtotal	$ 86,000 (0.02%)[a]	$ 178,000	$ 264,000[b]
Grand Total	$73,829,000 (27.1%)[a]	$162,857,000	$236,686,000[c]

[a]Percent of revenues raised from local sources.

[b]Although Boston spent $57,000 on air pollution control, if the state assumed financial responsibility, it would spend only $14,000 to deliver exactly the same services because of federal 3-for-1 matching provisions. Thus, state assumption of air pollution control costs would save municipalities $264,000 and would cost the state only $221,000.

[c]Because of the air pollution control item (see footnote a), this figure, which represents the total savings to municipalities resulting from shifting to the state, is not equal to the cost to the state of such a shift. The cost to the state is $236,643,000.

Table 6-2. Projected Expenditures on Boston Municipal Services Recommended for Shifting to State: 1973

Function and Service	City of Boston	All Municipalities Excluding Boston	All Municipalities	State Totals with Changes in Service Levels
Public Safety	$ 4,124,000	$5,669,000	$ 9,793,000	$ 9,793,000
Transportation				
Street maintenance	—[a]	—[a]	—[a]	$93,289,000
Public transit	34,601,000	41,566,000	76,167,000	76,376,000
Waste Disposal				
Solid waste	2,398,000	22,043,000	24,441,000	24,441,000
Sewage	7,509,000	10,848,000	18,357,000	18,357,000
County Courts & Corrections				
Courts	8,626,000	23,051,000	31,677,000	31,877,000
Corrections	3,435,000	7,583,000	11,018,000	14,470,000
Veterans Assistance	4,344,000	14,680,000	19,024,000	1,670,000
Health & Hospitals				
Municipal	13,214,000	16,812,000	30,026,000	30,026,000
School	914,000	4,330,000	5,244,000	5,244,000
County hospital assessments	—	2,354,000	2,354,000	2,354,000
Regional Parks & Recreation	6,984,000	22,834,000	29,818,000	29,818,000
Vocational Education	1,800,000	18,200,000	20,000,000	22,270,000
Regional Library Services	2,450,000	—	2,450,000	2,950,000
Air Pollution Control	96,000	198,000	294,000	247,000
Grand Total	$90,495,000	$190,168,000	$280,663,000	$363,182,000

[a]Municipal highway and highway-related expenditures from local funds are covered by Chapter 497 state aid enacted in 1971.

state expenditures. Under the first, and assuming leveling-up, approximately $93.2 million of the overall increase was allocated to the state motor fuel tax and $135 million each to the state income and sales taxes. This proposal would mean an increase of four cents per gallon in the motor fuel tax, and an increase of five percent in the sales tax. As for the income tax component, in order to make incidence calculations, the assumption was made that the additional funds would be raised by levying a surcharge on present state income tax bills, rather than inferring what kind of tax rate and tax base configurations might be designed to generate the additional revenues. This would mean a tax surcharge of 18 percent on present tax bills.

The tax arrangement under the second alternative is also $93.2 million for the motor fuel tax, while the remainder of the $270 million is allocated to the income tax. This additional income tax levy is equivalent to a surcharge of 36 percent on current state income tax bills.

In the no-leveling-up case (1970 expenditures), it is assumed that either (1) the Boston property tax is reduced by $73.8 million, the sales and income taxes are each increased by $110 million, and the motor fuel excise is raised by $15.9 million; or (2) the Boston property tax is reduced by $73.8 million, the state income tax is increased by $220 million, and the state motor fuel excise rises by $15.9 million.

Shifting to Three State Taxes

Consider first the case of no-leveling-up and a switch to the combination of state income, sales, and motor fuel taxes. Of the total Boston property tax reduction of $73.8 million, only 64 percent, or $47 million, is borne by local residents. In terms of state government taxes, Boston residents in 1970 contributed 20 percent of the state income tax, 8 percent of the sales tax, and 6 percent of the gasoline tax, mainly because they have lower average incomes and less consumption per family than the rest of the state. So a financing shift from local property taxes to *any* combination of these other state taxes *must* result in a lower aggregate total tax burden on Boston residents. In this case there will be a total state tax increase on Boston residents of $23.1 million, which will be more than offset by the reduction in property taxes of $47 million. This leaves a net reduction in taxes paid by Boston residents of $23.9 million. Hence, by shifting financing for selected municipal services to state government taxes without making adjustments for service levels and price changes, the *total state and local tax burden* on Boston residents can be reduced by about 10 percent.

A similar result is obtained if we consider a shift to these three state taxes on the basis of projected 1973 expenditures, including those expenditure changes resulting from service-level increases. As summarized in Table 6-2, total Boston expenditures in 1973 for the functions under discussion in this study are estimated to be over $90 million or about 32 percent of the statewide total on these functions. In this case, taxes paid by Boston residents would fall by a net of $24.9 million, that is, by 53 percent of current property tax payments.

The distribution of the tax burden among families is changed by the shift from the regressive property tax to the less regressive financing package. Changes in payments per dollar of income by income class are shown in Table 6-3. These results show a marked progressive effect on the distribution of tax burdens, and also show an absolute decline in tax burdens at all income levels. It is interesting to note that even when service-level adjustments are allowed, all Boston residents experience tax relief.[b]

---

[b]However, when changes in tax burdens are estimated by family size as well as income class, it is found that some households actually pay more tax after the shift: unrelated individuals with economic incomes greater than $25,000, on the average, would be liable for increased taxes.

Table 6-3. Changes in Taxes per Dollar of Economic Income Resulting from a Shift of Boston's Service-Package Financing to the State Government (in cents per dollar of income).

	Shift to State Income, Sales, and Motor Fuel Tax		*Shift to State Income and Motor Fuel Tax*	
Income Class	*1970 with no leveling-up*	*1973 with leveling-up*	*1970 with no leveling-up*	*1973 with leveling-up*
$0 - 999	–	–	–	–
1,000 - 1,999	−5.26¢	−6.07¢	−5.42¢	−6.27¢
2,000 - 2,999	−3.76	−4.32	−3.98	−4.60
3,000 - 3,999	−2.66	−3.04	−2.92	−3.35
4,000 - 4,999	−2.07	−2.35	−2.34	−2.68
5,000 - 5,999	−1.80	−2.04	−1.94	−2.20
6,000 - 6,999	−1.52	−1.69	−1.57	−1.75
7,000 - 7,999	−1.16	−1.23	−1.00	−1.04
8,000 - 8,999	−1.03	−1.05	−0.89	−0.88
9,000 - 9,999	−0.92	−0.92	−0.77	−0.73
10,000 - 11,999	−0.76	−0.72	−0.64	−0.58
12,000 - 14,999	−0.65	−0.59	−0.48	−0.39
14,000 - 24,999	−0.43	−0.37	−0.17	−0.05
25,000 and over	−0.29	−0.27	−0.11	−0.22

Shifting to Two State Taxes

As pointed out above, any shift from local property tax finance to state taxes must result in a decrease in the total tax burden on Boston residents. Because Boston residents pay a higher share of the total state income tax than of the sales tax, the shift discussed in this section results in less aggregate tax liability reduction than does the shift to all three taxes. The change in burdens among income classes is also different. Assuming no service-level increases, net total payments by Boston residents are reduced by $19.5 million. If service-level increases are assumed, net resident tax liabilities will fall by only slightly less.

The distribution of the above net reduction across income classes is more progressive than is the shift that included the sales tax. The highest income class would actually pay more taxes after the shift than before, and the average effective rate decreases at a more rapid rate toward the top of the income scale (see Table 6-3).[c]

---

[c]More detailed results show that in the over-$25,000 economic income class, all families of three or fewer members would pay more total taxes after the shift; in the $12,000-$25,000 range, "unrelated individuals" would also experience tax increases.

KANSAS CITY[3]

The single function considered for shifting in the Kansas City study is education, with the effects evaluated in the case of both the Kansas City, Kansas and Kansas City, Missouri central cities.[d] Any plans for functional reassignment in this SMSA are complicated by the highly fragmented nature of SMSA governance—particularly the two-state feature. There are 272 local jurisdictions within the Kansas City metropolitan area, broken down as follows:

	Missouri	Kansas	Total
Counties	4	2	6
Municipalities	63	22	85
Townships	18	14	32
Special Districts	34	23	57
School Districts	69	23	97
Totals	188	84	272

In terms of fiscal operations, the most significant jurisdictions within the SMSA are the two central cities, the two central counties, and the two central-city school districts. These six basic units account for approximately 54 percent of total SMSA expenditures (1972). If we add to this number the expenditures of the other 90 school districts, the total accounted for rises to about 83 percent. In other words, the remaining 176 local governments (4 counties, 83 municipalities, 32 townships, and 57 special districts) account for only 17 percent of all local expenditures. The problem is complicated further by the two-state feature, a constraint that tends to thwart even the simplest effort at intergovernmental cooperation to attack common metropolitan problems, such as the formation of an integrated public transit system.[4]

Alternative assumptions were made about the leveling-up issue, though state-wide equalization of expenditures per student was assumed in every case. First, it is assumed that after state assumption, education spending per pupil (net of federal aids) remains at the current level of approximately $575. Under the second alternative, the level is allowed to rise to $650. The financing of the increased state expenditure responsibility is assumed to come partially from a new state property tax of one dollar per hundred of valuation *applied only to residential property*. The remainder of the necessary increment in state financing would come from one of four alternative financing schemes. Under *Proposal 1*, the remainder of the school operating expenses are funded entirely from an increase in the state sales tax; *Proposal 2* places the full burden of

---

[d]The Kansas City report also considered the shifting of welfare, but only the education case is presented here.

incremental financing upon the state income tax. Proposals 3 and 4 are mid-positions to the first two alternatives, and as such may actually be more politic-cally acceptable. *Proposal 3,* in general, gives a greater relative weight to the income tax than to the sales tax, while *Proposal 4* does the reverse. In all cases it is assumed that local property tax relief is only in the form of *residential* rate reduction; business property tax rates are not changed.

For Missouri the replacement of the local educational property tax with a 10 mill state levy leaves a deficit statewide of $163 million when per student expenditures are increased to $650. Under Proposal 1, this deficit may be offset by an increase in the sales tax to 4.25 percent (up from 3 percent). Alternatively, the deficit may be counterbalanced by Proposal 2, which changes the state income tax to have marginal rates ranging from 3.75 percent (under-$1,000 taxable income) to 8.25 percent (over-$9,000 taxable income). Either of these methods would generate sufficient revenue to cover the increased state educational expenditures.

Proposal 3, on the other hand, generates sufficient revenue to off-set the property tax reduction by raising the marginal income tax rates to 1.5 percent for the under-$1,000 income class, to 6 percent for taxable incomes over $9,000, and by increasing the sales tax rate by 0.75 percent. In Proposal 3, in relative terms, 60 percent of the funds are to come from the state income tax and 40 percent from the state sales tax. Proposal 4, on the other hand, places 58 percent of the burden of financing on the state sales tax and 42 percent on the state income tax.

In the case of Kansas City, Kansas, replacement of the school property levy would require an estimated $93.9 million in additional state revenues to fund public school expenditures at the $650 per pupil level. Like Missouri, the increased revenues may be generated either by an increase in the state sales tax or by revisions in the state income tax. If the sales tax solution is elected, the rate would jump from 3 percent to 5 percent—not an abnormal level by comparison with many states.

Proposal 3, as applied in Kansas, places more emphasis on the financing of education by the income tax. Marginal income tax rates are pro-gressively raised from 3 percent for the lowest class to 8 percent for the over-$14,000 bracket, while the state sales tax is raised to 4.25 percent. Of the total of $95.8 million estimated from these changes, 37 percent is attributable to the income tax. As stated, Proposal 4 is slightly more dependent upon sales tax revenues. The existing 3 percent sales tax rate is raised to 4.38 percent, and the income tax schedule is revised upward from a low of 2 percent in the bottom class to 7.5 percent in the top class. Revenues from the sales tax amount to 70 percent of the total yield from the two sources.

The net impact of the four alternative financing proposals on the net tax liability of the individual central cities is described in Table 6-4. Although the preceding discussion is based on an equalization expenditure of $650 per

Table 6-4. Net Tax Liabilities Incurred by Residents of Kansas City, Missouri and Kansas City, Kansas following Educational Expenditure Shifts (thousands of dollars).

	State Equalization of $575 per ADA	State Equalization of $650 per ADA
Proposal 1		
Kansas City, Kansas	−$247	+$673
Kansas City, Missouri	−10,117	−8,652
Proposal 2		
Kansas City, Kansas	−206	+2,160
Kansas City, Missouri	−775	+5,024
Proposal 3		
Kansas City, Kansas	−499	−954
Kansas City, Missouri	−3,746	−829
Proposal 4		
Kansas City, Kansas	−436	+299
Kansas City, Missouri	−11,570	−3,141

pupil, the same type of analysis would apply for other assumed values, for example, $575, as is illustrated in Table 6-4. The figures shown in Table 6-4 are determined by applying the statewide rates of the various proposals directly to the observed tax liabilities of the individual cities. For example, replacing the local school levy with the statewide 10 mill levy reduces the property tax liability of Kansas City, Missouri residents by $15,946,000 (from $37,970,000 to $22,024,000) and the residents of Kansas City, Kansas by $3,005,000 (from $14,893,000 to $11,888,000). Following Proposal 1 ($650), which places the increased tax solely on retail sales, total sales tax payments increase by $7,294,000 in Kansas City, Missouri and by $3,678,000 in adjacent Kansas City, Kansas. The net result is a $8,652,000 *decrease* in overall tax payments for residents of Kansas City, Missouri, but a net *increase* of $673,000 for residents in the sister city. In a similar manner the remaining entries in Table 6-4 are calculated.

Several interesting results emerge from a comparison of the alternative financing schemes. First, although not explicitly shown in Table 6-4, the proposals that place more weight on the retail sales tax in the alternative proposals for financing education tend to improve the net tax liability position of the two urban areas more than do the proposals that favor the income tax. The Kansas City study suggests that this finding is due in part to the fact that retail sales taxes are partially shifted to out-of-state residents, so not all of the required educational revenues must be paid by state residents. In contrast, personal income taxes are not shiftable. The education revenues, therefore, must come from the taxable income of the respective states, a significant portion of which is concentrated in the two urban areas under consideration.

Second, at the assumed per pupil aid level of $575, all four proposals result in a reduction of the aggregate tax burden in the two central cities. With the increase in the ADA level to $650, the situation changes. In Kansas City, Kansas, none of the proposals provides a decrease in total taxes, while on the Missouri side of the line, only Proposal 2 (total reliance upon the state income tax) results in a tax increase. But even in the case of Kansas City, Missouri, the absolute amount of the net decrease in taxes is diminished. The implication stemming from these observations is that any plan to shift educational expenditures to the state level will tend to shift the burden of the taxes toward suburban and out-of-state residents, i.e., away from the central city residents.

Third, the sales tax is a more potent revenue resource in both states than is the income tax. The increase in tax rates is considerably less for the sales tax than the income tax. This is not surprising, however, given that part of the retail sales tax revenues are paid by individuals and businesses outside the state, and state income taxes frequently allow large deductions from adjusted gross income.

Distribution of Total
Tax Burden after the Education Shift

A fundamental consideration in the four alternative financing schemes is the impact of the changes on the distribution of income and the degree of progessivity in average tax rates for individual families. Changes in effective tax rates for a family of four under Proposals 1 and 2 are shown in Table 6-5, separately for each city, and assuming equalization of per student expenditures at $650. In general the conclusions and trends drawn for families of four are similar to those for families of other sizes.

Consider first the results for Kansas City, Missouri. While the sales tax alternative reduces the average tax rates on individuals and families of all sizes, the proposal does little to change the rates of progression in the total tax system. The income tax proposal, however, does noticeably change the degree of average rate progression. As may be seen in Table 6-5, the income tax increase will increase family tax burdens only for families with incomes above $10,000.

The situation in Kansas City, Kansas is markedly different. Under the sales tax proposal, family tax liabilities increase at all income levels except the lowest. The sales tax thus seems to hit large, low-income families harder than does the existing property tax. The income tax proposal, on the other hand, appears to increase the average rate of progression for both individuals and families.

Table 6-5. **Changes in Taxes per Dollar of Economic Income Resulting from a Shift of Kansas City's Education Financing to the State Governments (in cents per dollar of income).**

| | Proposal 1[a] | | Proposal 2[b] | |
| | Kansas City, | Kansas City, | Kansas City, | Kansas City, |
Income Class	Kansas	Missouri	Kansas	Missouri
$0 - 999	-3.47¢	-7.46¢	-4.56¢	-8.15¢
1,000 - 1,999	0.13	-1.51	-0.88	-2.11
2,000 - 2,999	0.23	-0.89	-0.73	-1.48
3,000 - 3,999	0.37	-0.54	-0.61	-1.13
4,000 - 4,999	0.33	-0.35	-0.58	-0.88
5,000 - 5,999	0.38	-0.27	-0.25	-0.68
6,000 - 6,999	0.46	-0.30	0.04	-0.54
7,000 - 7,999	0.46	-0.29	0.21	-0.31
8,000 - 8,999	0.50	-0.30	0.37	-0.21
9,000 - 9,999	0.50	-0.29	0.46	-0.09
10,000 - 11,999	0.24	-0.27	0.25	0.11
12,000 - 14,999	0.09	-0.35	0.35	0.13
15,000 - 24,999	-0.48	-0.43	0.11	0.38
25,000 and over	0.49	-0.27	0.78	0.43

[a]State property and state sales tax.
[b]State property and state income tax.

A comparison of the changes in average rates resulting from expenditure shifting in the two states can be summarized as follows:

1. While aggregate tax increases under the sales tax option are less than under the income tax in both cities, the retail sales tax tends to be more regressive in Kansas City, Kansas, than the income tax option. For Kansas City, Missouri, the sales tax proposal leads to an across-the-board decrease in taxes.

2. An increase in state income taxes leads in both cities to an increase in average rate progressions.

3. Under either proposal, average rates for households in the same income classes and family sizes will be higher in Kansas City, Kansas than in Kansas City, Missouri, despite the latter's 0.5 percent earnings tax. This result is most probably explained by reference to the respective state economic bases. Kansas, with a more agrarian tax base, derives a larger portion of its revenue from the few large cities in the state. Missouri's economic base is semi-industrialized and has more urban areas to share the tax burdens, thereby reducing any one area's relative burden.

4. Neither proposal in either state will reduce the relative regressivity in average rate for persons up to approximately $5,000 in income. It might be suggested that this problem could best be handled by sales tax and property tax rebates to households in the lower income classes.

5. In both states, those households with income exceeding $25,000 pay pro-
portionately lower rates than those households with incomes between
$10,000 and $25,000. In the absence of extremely high marginal income
tax rates in the highest taxable income bracket, it is doubtful that any
feasible tax change would alter these results.

SAN DIEGO[5]

San Diego is far from the point of a fiscal crisis.[6] Still, longer-term considerations suggest the potential value of a reassignment of functions. Two forms of
functional reassignment are considered for the San Diego metropolitan area:
county assumption of a package consisting of eight central-city functions, and
state assumption of all education financing.

Using as guidelines the ACIR's general criteria for functional responsibility and political feasibility, the San Diego UO selected eight functions
that might be better financed at the county level. In total, these eight functions
accounted for $4.68 million in the 1969-1970 budget, or an amount equivalent
to 7 percent of locally raised revenues, about $6.72 per capita. In addition, if
the state were to assume full responsibility for education finance, it is estimated
that for fiscal 1969-1970 the central city would have transferred $52.7 million
or $76 per capita in education expenditures to the state.

The financing schemes involved include shifting the finance of the
service package from a city to a county property tax, and shifting education
finance from a school district property tax to a combination of a new 2 percent
state sales tax and an income tax surcharge of 153 percent.

County Assumption of the Service Package

The data in Table 6-6 show the expenditures and revenues associated with the eight functions being considered. The city/suburban disparities in
revenues specifically available for these functions (see Table 6-6) indicate a
source of potential opposition to such a shift. While the central city spends
$10.9 million on these functions, its user-charge revenues and the like, collected
in connection with the functions, amount to only $6.3 million. On the other
hand, local governments in the county, but outside central city, spend $2.9
million on the service package, but have revenues from these functions of $3.9
million. This means that should the outside-central-city portion of the county
agree to countywide financing, they would lose a $1 million revenue surplus on
these functions.

By shifting the service package to the county, the city could reduce
net expenditures by $4.6 million, while the outside-central-city taxpayers would
shift $1 million in net revenues to the regional government. On balance, then,
the regional government would have to raise an incremental amount of $4.6

Table 6-6. Expenditures and Revenues of Services Transferred to the County from San Diego and Other Local Governments in the Region.

Functions	Expenditures	Revenues
Crime Lab	$ 292,210	$ 4,000
San Diego	225,706	4,000
Other Cities	66,504	0
Mass Transit	7,042,183	5,747,776
San Diego System	6,431,632	5,016,984
Oceanside System	610,551	730,792
Airports	2,171,662	2,973,979
San Diego	331,662	223,979
Other (Port Authority)	1,840,000	2,750,000
Cultural Institutions	785,230	0
San Diego	767,211	0
Other Cities	18,019	0
Sanitary Fills	776,376	380,924
San Diego	620,114	17,624
Other Cities (Oceanside)	156,262	363,300
Flood Control	456,595	0
San Diego	359,145	0
Other Cities	97,450	0
Stadium (San Diego only)	2,170,805	964,574
Business License Enforcement	183,618	183,618
San Diego	70,000	70,000
Other Cities	113,618	113,618
Total	$13,968,679	$10,254,871
San Diego	10,976,275	6,297,161
Other	2,902,404	3,957,710

million minus $1 million, or $3.6 million. The analysis is worked out on the basis of no-levelling-up of expenditures.

The data in Table 6-7 show that the net amount of property tax reduction experienced by residents of San Diego is $3.9 million. This implies that $700,000 in property taxes, or 15.1 percent of total property tax revenues, is exported in the form of higher prices. On the other hand, of the $3.6 million in new regional property taxes to be raised on a countywide basis, San Diego residents would bear only $1.5 million of the total. On balance, then, San Diego residents would decrease their aggregate property tax burden by $2.4 million.

The effect of this net tax reduction on representative families in different income classes is shown in Table 6-8. All families experience tax

Table 6–7. Aggregate Tax Liability Effects on San Diego Residents Resulting from Shifting Financing of the Service Package from the Local Property Tax to a Regional Property Tax (millions of dollars)

Net Effect on Budget of City Government:

1. Expenditures shifted	$10.9
2. Revenues shifted	6.3
3. Net change in financing required	−4.6

Effect on Residents:

1. Net expenditure amount shifted to county	$4.6
2. Resident property tax reduction[a]	3.9
3. Aggregate amount to be financed by county government[b]	3.6
4. Net amount of property taxes to be raised by county[a]	3.0
5. Amount of (4) paid by San Diego residents from the regional property tax	1.5
6. Aggregate tax liability change to San Diego residents	−2.4

[a]It is estimated that 15.1 percent of property taxes are exported.
[b]One million dollars in existing user-charges accounts for the difference between the figure and total financing required.

Table 6–8. Changes in Taxes per Dollar of Economic Income Resulting from a Shift of San Diego's Service-Package Financing to a Regional Property Tax (in cents per dollar of Income)

Income Class

$0 - 999	−0.20¢
1,000 - 1,999	−0.12
2,000 - 2,999	−0.09
3,000 - 3,999	−0.07
4,000 - 4,999	−0.07
5,000 - 5,999	−0.07
6,000 - 6,999	−0.06
7,000 - 7,999	−0.06
8,000 - 8,999	−0.06
9,000 - 9,999	−0.06
10,000 - 11,999	−0.05
12,000 - 14,999	−0.05
15,000 - 24,999	−0.04
25,000 and over	−0.03

reductions under the county assumption scheme proposed here. However, while families in the lower income classes ($3,000-$4,000) experience tax decreases of 0.07 cents per dollar of economic income, families in the highest income bracket ($25,000 and over) experience tax decreases of only 0.03 cents per dollar of economic income. This slight reduction in the overall regressivity of

the burden distribution among central-city residents is due solely to a net reduction in total central-city property tax liability. However, because of the small
amount of expenditures involved, the changes in effective rates are very slight.

Shifting Education Finance to the State

If the state of California assumed financial responsibility for education, then it would incur $2.339 billion in new expenditures for fiscal 1969-
1970 if no leveling-up is assumed. This increase was distributed between the
state sales taxes and income taxes in the following manner: first, the state sales
tax rate was increased by 2 percent, generating an estimated $578.6 million
dollars in 1969-1970. The residual, $1.76 billion, is raised from a state income
tax surcharge of 153 percent. Again, no leveling-up is assumed.

The data in Table 6-9 show that state financial assumption would reduce school property taxes collected in San Diego by $52.7 million. Of this
amount, it is estimated that city residents pay directly or indirectly $44.7
million. This is the amount of gross property tax relief provided to city residents. However, the state would need to finance $2.3 billion in new education
expenditures if it assumed responsibility for all local education costs. Assuming

Table 6–9. **Aggregate Tax Liability Effects on San Diego Residents
Resulting from Shifting Education Financing to a Combination of
the State Personal Income and Sales Taxes (millions of dollars)**

Effect on the City and State Budgets:	
Amount of school property taxes raised in San Diego (1969)	$ 52.7
Aggregate local school expenditures assumed by state	2,339.4
Effect on Residents of San Diego:	
School property tax reduction to San Diego residents[a]	44.7
New state sales taxes paid by San Diego residents	12.7
New state income taxes paid by San Diego residents	52.8
Total new state sales and income taxes paid by San Diego residents	65.5
Aggregate increase in taxes paid by residents of San Diego	20.8

[a]Again, as in the case of the service package, 15.1 percent of property taxes are assumed
to be exported.

that the state decided to levy a 2 percent increase in the sales tax and finance
the residual by an income tax surcharge, it is estimated that San Diego residents would incur $12.7 million in new sales taxes and $52.8 million in new
income taxes. In total, the new state taxes raised for education from San Diego
residents would be $65.5 million or an amount $20.8 million greater than their
original tax burden of $44.7 million. Hence, aggregate tax liability would rise
by about 45 percent of existing education property tax liability.

The interpersonal equity effects of such a shift, shown in Table
6-10, reveal a progressive effect of this financial shift. Examination of these data

Table 6-10. Changes in Taxes per Dollar of Economic Income Resulting from a Shift of San Diego's Education Financing to a Combination of a 2 Percent State Sales Tax and a 153 Percent Surcharge on the State Income Tax (in cents per dollar of income)

Income Class	
$0 - 999	−5.9¢
1,000 - 1,999	−3.4
2,000 - 2,999	−2.6
3,000 - 3,999	−2.1
4,000 - 4,999	−1.6
5,000 - 5,999	−1.1
6,000 - 6,999	−0.8
7,000 - 7,999	−0.5
8,000 - 8,999	−0.3
9,000 - 9,999	−0.2
10,000 - 11,999	0.1
12,000 - 14,999	0.6
15,000 - 24,999	1.5
25,000 and over	2.1

shows that while families in the lower income classes ($3,000-$4,000, for example) experience tax decreases of 2.1 cents per dollar of economic income, families in the middle-income range ($12,000-$15,000) experience tax increases of 0.6 cents per dollar of economic income, and families in the highest income class experience tax increases of 2.1 cents per dollar of income. The different equity effects experienced by low-income families versus high-income families is attributed to the shift from the regressive property tax to the less regressive mix of sales and income taxes.

BALTIMORE[7]

The Baltimore study is focused on the equity and budgetary consequences of state government assumption of education finance in Maryland. The reasons for studying only the education function are persuasive. Elementary and secondary education is by far the most costly program carried out at the local level. Locally financed education absorbs more than 47 percent of local taxes in the Baltimore SMSA. If we consider property taxes alone, the figure increases to 68 percent. Thus the potential for relief is greater in this area than for any other locally financed service.[8]

Several forms of education financing reforms are considered in the Baltimore study. For purposes of this analysis, only two—dealing with state financial assumption—are considered.[e] Under the first, full state financial as-

---

[e]The Baltimore study makes a persuasive case for an increased and reformed state aid program as an alternative superior to state financial assumption.

sumption would raise per pupil spending to the statewide average of $957 (Baltimore presently spends $938). The second would equalize statewide per pupil expenditures at $1,079.

The two state financial assumption schemes studied here call for the local income tax to revert to the state and for local property taxes to fall by an amount equal to the difference between locally raised school expenditures and local income tax receipts. The increased state expenditures are considered as being financed alternatively from state income, sales, and property taxes, with the following effective rate increases implied: for the lower cost alternative, 3.78 percent on the income tax, $0.97 per $1,000 of market valuation under the property tax, and 5.17 percent under the sales tax; for the higher cost alternative, the effective rate increases are 5.11 percent, $1.31 per $1,000 of market valuation, and 6.99 percent, respectively. The magnitude of such rate increases makes it clear that some combination of the three taxes will be necessary to make such financing reform politically acceptable, it simply would not, for example, be politically feasible to raise the sales tax rate by 7 percent.

The effects of full state financing under either cost assumption or either financing assumption would be to increase the aggregate tax burden on Baltimore residents. In fiscal 1969-1970, Baltimore raised $147 million in property taxes and $27.8 million from the piggyback income tax. The assumption made in the Baltimore study is that shifting education financing to the state government would force the local governments to give up the piggyback income tax; that is, it is assumed that political realities would dictate state takeover of the piggyback income tax option because of the increased state government resources required.

The data in Table 6-11 summarize the aggregate effects of shifting education finance from the city property tax to the state income tax under the lower cost state program. These results show that of the $48.8 million of local property tax financed education expenditures, only about three-fourths, or $36.4 million, is borne by Baltimore residents. The remaining one-fourth is exported to residents outside of Baltimore. On the other hand the state government, in assuming all local education costs, would incur $306 million net in new expenditure responsibility. Of this amount, it is estimated that Baltimore residents would incur new income tax liabilities of over $52 million. On balance, then, the aggregate tax payments of Baltimore's residents would increase by $15.9 million or $17.60 per capita. With sales tax financing, there is a net increase of $24.8 million or $27.50 per Baltimore City resident.

If the analogous computations are made for the higher cost program, the tax burden on city residents rises by $34.4 million or $38.13 per capita under the income tax, and by $46.4 million or $51.43 per capita under the sales tax. In sum, there is a leveling-up effect under either program, and in each case the aggregate tax burden on Baltimore residents rises substantially. The tax burden effects described in Table 6-12 show that income tax finance results

Table 6-11. Aggregate Tax Liability Effects on Baltimore Residents Resulting from Shifting Education Financing to the State Income or Sales Tax (millions of dollars).

	Income Tax Financing	Sales Tax Financing
1. Locally raised revenues for education	$76.6	$76.6
2. Amount of (1) from piggyback income tax	27.8	27.8
3. Aggregate amount financed by the local property tax (1-2)	48.8	48.8
4. Amount of (3) borne by residents of Baltimore (48.8 X 0.746)	36.4	36.4
5. Sum of all local education cost assumed by the state	500.0	500.0
6. Sum of all local piggyback income taxes	194.0	194.0
7. Amount to be raised from new state tax	306.0	306.0
8. Amount of (7) raised from residents of Baltimore	52.3	61.2
9. Net increase in taxes on Baltimore residents	15.9	24.8
10. Per capita net increase in taxes on Baltimore residents (in dollars)	17.60	27.50

Table 6-12. Changes in Taxes per Dollar of Economic Income Resulting from a Shift of Baltimore's Education Financing to State Sales or Personal Income Taxation (in cents per dollar of income).

Income Class	Income Tax Financing	Sales Tax Financing
$ 0 - 2,999	−3.998¢	−1.332¢
3,000 - 4,999	−1.454	0.287
5,000 - 6,999	−1.022	0.331
7,000 - 9,999	−0.196	0.306
10,000 - 14,999	0.394	0.315
15,000 - 24,999	0.842	0.291
25,000 and over	1.184	0.792

in a redistribution from upper to lower income brackets, even after account is taken of the leveling-up effects. All families with incomes below $10,000 benefit from absolute tax burden reductions. Sales tax financing, on the other hand, provides a tax reduction for only the lowest income class.

DENVER[9]

A recent fiscal study of Denver SMSA governments concluded that serious deficits could be expected by 1976, and that revenue-sharing will not bridge the projected revenue-expenditure gap.[10] Faced with this prospect, the Denver study evaluated the consequences of fiscal centralization on the city/county and its residents, as a means of alleviating this expected fiscal squeeze.

Using the ACIR criteria, judgment, and political feasibility considerations as guides, nine functions were selected as candidates for shifting to regional authorities. In addition, the effects of shifting the welfare function from the city/county of Denver to the state were studied.

The city/county of Denver provides a number of important services whose benefits spill over to the entire five-county metropolitan area. Of all such functions, those that impose the most substantial financing requirements on the central city were selected as possible candidates for shifting to a broader regional authority. There is a legal basis for such a regional authority: Colorado voters, in 1969, approved a constitutional amendment that enlarged the options available for metropolitan government by allowing for the formation of regional service authorities.

The financial importance of these nine services is outlined in Table 6-13. The functions to be shifted to county financing account for 7.9 percent of revenues raised from local sources, and welfare expenditures (exclusive of aids) account for another 6.8 percent. Thus, shifting the service package and welfare to higher levels of government would free up, for tax reduction or expenditure on other functions, 14.7 percent of the total city budget, or $32 per capita.

For the shifting of the service package to a regional authority, two financing alternatives were considered: a shift to a regional property tax and a

Table 6-13. Expenditures from Own Sources[a] on Candidate Functions for Regional and State Financial Assumptions: 1969-1970.

Function	Expenditure	Percent
Service Package		
Art Museum	$ 337,800	0.3%
Natural History Museum	363,900	0.3
Botanical Gardens	947,939	0.8
Zoological Gardens	466,400	0.4
Public Library	3,052,900	2.8
Denver Metro-Transit	500,000	0.5
Secondary Roads	667,795	0.6
Prisons	2,433,301	2.2
Total for Service Package	8,780,035	7.9
Welfare	7,548,000	6.8
Total	$16,328,035	14.7%

[a]This is the amount spent from the Denver (City/County) general fund after netting out any private contributions, state and federal aids and user fees.

shift to a regional sales tax. For the shifting of welfare financing to the state government, two financing alternatives were considered: a shift to a state income tax and a shift to a state sales tax.

It is estimated that the shift of this service package to a regional base will result in an overall expenditure increase because of a leveling-up effect. On a function-by-function basis, the following four considerations lead to an estimate of this expenditure increase:

1. A citizen attitude survey of cultural facilities usage indicates that service levels are thought to be high enough and, therefore, no additional expenditures are expected because of reorganization.
2. Regionalization of Metro Transit services would increase costs by 40 percent. The increase is due primarily to route expansions.
3. Expenditures on secondary roads would increase by $20,000 per year.
4. Consolidation of all prison facilities would double expenditures on correctional programs.

The effects of leveling-up on the expenditures for the service package are summarized in Table 6-14. In total, the expenditures on these functions were estimated to increase from $8.7 million to $11.4 million.

Shifting Financing of the Service Package

It is estimated that the net savings to the Denver city budget of shifting the service package would be $8.7 million. The tax savings to city residents, from this shift, would be less, however, since some locally raised taxes are exported. In the case of Denver's property tax, since 44.1 percent of assessed

Table 6-14. Expenditures in 1969-1970 by the City/County of Denver on Selected Functions, and Hypothesized Expenditure if the Functions Were Provided by a Regional Authority

Function	*Expenditure 1970*	*Estimated 1970 Expenditures if Provided by a Regional Base*
Art Museum	$ 337,800	$ 337,800
Natural History Museum	363,900	363,900
Botanical Gardens	957,939	957,939
Zoological Gardens	466,400	466,400
Public Library	3,052,900	3,052,900
Metro-Transit	500,000	700,000
Secondary Roads	677,795	697,795
Prisons	2,433,302	4,866,607
Total	$8,780,035	$11,433,336

value is residential, it is assumed that city residents would experience direct property tax savings of that proportion of the total $8.7 million reduction, or $3.8 million. A further savings to residents is the 37.8 percent of $3.2 million in nonresidential property taxes estimated to be borne by city residents in the form of higher prices. The sum of these direct plus indirect property taxes, $7 million, is the gross amount of property tax savings that city residents would initially experience (see Table 6-15).

On the other hand, reorganization and leveling-up mean that the county must levy a property tax to cover the higher cost of $11.4 million. Based on its share of assessed value, Denver residents will bear $4.7 million of this total. City residents are estimated to pay $2.5 million in direct property taxes and $2.2 million in indirect property taxes, or a total of $4.7 million. Hence, the net property tax savings to Denver residents from such a shift is $2.3 million, or about $4.40 per capita. If the county levied a new sales tax to raise the $11.4 million, it is estimated that 15 percent, or $1.7 million, would be exported (mainly due to the tourist industry in the Denver area) to residents outside Colorado (see Table 6-16). Of the remaining $9.7 million raised from residents of the region, it was estimated that 52 percent, or $5 million, would be borne by Denver's residents. On balance, then, residents of Denver would have incurred an aggregate tax decrease of $3.2 million had this type of regionalization been enacted in fiscal 1969-1970.

The effect of this financing shift on Denver residents, if a county property tax is used, is to decrease tax burdens at all income levels (see Table 6-17). This is a consequence of the reduction in the absolute amount of total

Table 6-15. Aggregate Tax Liability Effects on Denver Budget and Denver Residents of Shifting the Service Package to a Regional Property Tax (millions of dollars).

Net City Budget Reduction	$ 8.7
Effect on City Residents:	
Direct Denver residential property taxes	3.8
Indirect Denver residential property taxes	3.2
Total direct and indirect Denver property taxes	7.0
New Regional Taxes Necessary	11.4
Effect on Denver Residents:	
Direct residential taxes paid to regional authority by Denver residents	2.5
Indirect residential taxes paid to regional authority by Denver residents	2.2
Total	4.7
Net Cost to Denver Residents of Shifting	−$ 2.3

Table 6-16. Aggregate Tax Liability Effects on Denver Budget and Denver Residents of Shifting the Service Package to a Regional Sales Tax (millions of dollars).

Net City Budget Reduction	$ 8.7
Effect on City Residents:	
Direct Denver residential property taxes	3.8
Indirect Denver residential property taxes	3.2
Total direct and indirect Denver property tax reduction	7.0
New Regional Taxes Necessary	11.4
Net Effect on Denver Residents:	
New sales tax paid by Denver residents (0.5%)	5.0
Net cost to Denver residents	−$ 3.2

Table 6-17. Changes in Taxes per Dollar of Economic Income Resulting from Shifting Denver's Service-Package Financing to County Taxes (in cents per dollar of income).

Income Class	Regional Property Tax	Regional Sales Tax
$0 - 999	−5.20¢	1.30¢
1,000 - 1,999	−0.19	0.08
2,000 - 2,999	−0.15	0.09
3,000 - 3,999	−0.12	0.09
4,000 - 4,999	−0.13	0.01
5,000 - 5,999	−0.11	0.00
7,000 - 6,999	−0.10	−0.01
7,000 - 7,999	−0.10	−0.01
8,000 - 8,999	−0.10	−0.06
9,000 - 9,999	−0.10	−0.05
10,000 - 11,999	−0.12	−0.13
12,000 - 14,999	−0.12	−0.13
15,000 - 24,999	−0.11	−0.17
25,000 and over	−0.04	−0.05

resources required from Denver residents. Naturally, families in the lower income classes experience more tax relief per dollar of economic income than families with high incomes because the property tax burden is regressive and because there is a larger than average proportion of the regional poor in Denver County. The case where there is no leveling-up, for instance, shows that families in the $4,000-$4,999 class experience tax relief of 0.13 cents per dollar of economic income, while families in the highest category gain relief of only 0.04 cents per dollar of economic income. In general, it might be concluded that the burden distribution changes are marginal.

As can be seen from the right column in Table 6-17, the effect on Denver residents of shifting financial responsibility to a regional sales tax differs from the property tax option, but again the effects are slight.

Shifting Welfare Financing to a State Income Tax

The shift from partial local financing of welfare cost with the property tax to full state government financing with the state income tax would reduce the welfare claim on local funds—an amount of $7.5 million. On the other hand, state assumption of all local welfare costs would raise total state government welfare expenditure by $18.7 million.

As shown in Table 6-18, under this shift the net reduction in property taxes paid for welfare by Denver residents would have been $6.1 million. On the other hand, of the $18.7 million in new state income taxes to be raised by the state government, $5.4 million would have come from Denver residents. On balance, city residents would have decreased their aggregate tax burdens by $700,000, or $1.40 per capita.

As can be seen in Table 6-19, the effect of shifting Denver's welfare financing from the local property tax to the state income tax is to decrease the tax burdens of all those with incomes below $15,000 and to increase the tax burdens for those families in income classes above $15,000. As in the case of some of the other cities studied, there is an interesting policy conclusion that results from shifting welfare financing to the state income tax: aggregate tax payments for Denver residents decrease, but the highest two income classes experienced tax increases. Again, however, it should be noted that the effects on the overall distribution of income are small in magnitude.

NASHVILLE–DAVIDSON[11]

Nashville-Davidson is free of many of the fiscal problems that typically press large central cities. There are many reasons for this relative fiscal health: a strong and growing economic base, a relatively small size (the SMSA population is 464,000), and, in general, a "new city" status that enables avoiding many of the stereotype urban problems. This relatively strong budgetary position is in no small measure also a result of discretionary public actions, the most important being a city-county consolidation in 1963. Whatever the reasons, a recent fiscal study had concluded that the current system of tax revenues will grow at a rate adequate to meet expenditure needs until the 1980s.[12] While the current rate of inflation may well hasten the appearance of this revenue gap, few large cities could have boasted of such fiscal strength, even two years ago.

Metropolitan Nashville, however, is not without fiscal problems. Three general issues stand out: a regressive distribution of state/local government tax burdens, a longer-term need to find a more income-elastic base for the financing of local services and the recognition that state government actions,

Table 6–18. Aggregate Tax Liability Effects of Shifting Welfare Financing to the State Income Tax (millions of dollars).

Net Effect on Denver City/County Budget	$ 7.5
Effect on City Residents·	
Direct Denver residential property taxes	3.3
Indirect Denver residential property taxes	2.8
Total direct and indirect Denver resident property tax reduction	6.1
New State Income Tax Necessary to Finance State Assumption of Welfare	18.7
Net Effect on Denver Residents:	
Aggregate new income tax liabilities of Denver residents	5.4
Aggregate net decrease in taxes to Denver residents	0.7

Table 6–19. Changes in Taxes per Dollar of Economic Income Resulting from Shifting Denver's Welfare Financing from the Local Property Tax to the State Income Tax (in cents per dollar of income).

Income Class	
$0 - 999	−14.02¢
1,000 - 1,999	−0.51
2,000 - 2,999	−0.40
3,000 - 3,999	−0.31
3,000 - 4,999	−0.31
5,000 - 5,999	−0.23
6,000 - 6,999	−0.18
7,000 - 7,999	−0.17
8,000 - 8,999	−0.15
9,000 - 9,999	−0.11
10,000 - 11,999	−0.15
12,000 - 14,999	−0.12
15,000 - 24,999	0.22
25,000 and over	0.08

now and in the future, are apt to be influenced by wide disparities in urban/rural public service levels. With these considerations in mind, the Nashville-Davidson UO studied the potential impact of state financial assumption of a set of urban functions.

Functions to be Shifted

As in other UO studies, a number of factors guided the choice of functions to be considered for state financial assumption. In the last analysis the final choice was based on judgment about spillovers, administrative considerations, the importance of local autonomy, and political feasibility considerations. The seven functions to be considered and the practicality of state financial assumption are outlined in columns 1 and 2 of Table 6-20. Nashville-Davidson expenditures on these functions amount to about $48 million or about $100 per capita.

Alternative assumptions are made about the leveling-up issue, that is, about the effects of state assumption on expenditure equalization and, therefore, on the level of total state government financing required. The three basic forms of leveling-up considered are (1) that expenditures continue at their present level, i.e., there is no leveling-up; (2) that statewide expenditures are equalized at the metropolitan level; and (3) that either no leveling-up or full equalization at the metropolitan level occurs but only 80 percent of total expenditures are so affected. The calculation methods are detailed in column 6 of Table 6-20.

Taxes to be Affected

The burden of state and local taxes in Tennessee is highly regressive. The only major tax that does not show a regressive pattern of effective rates is the very limited state personal income tax. But, the income tax is not considered a feasible tax to increase in the event of state financial assumption, and therefore the option appears to be to move toward reliance on more regressive tax forms. The equity of various taxes is summarized in this study in terms of Gini coefficients, which describe the divergence between percent of income earned and percent of taxes paid: with perfect equality, that population earning 10 percent of total income would pay 10 percent of total taxes, for example. A Gini coefficient less than unity would indicate a regressive tax—for instance, that population earning the lowest 10 percent of total income pays *more* than 10 percent of total taxes—and the lower the Gini coefficient, the more regressive the tax. Using this summary procedure, the pattern of state and local government tax burdens is about the same (0.715 and 0.722 respectively, which results in an overall coefficient of 0.7188).

It is assumed that increased state expenditures will be financed from some combination of increased state general sales taxes, auto license fees, and corporate excise (income) taxation, and that local property taxes will be reduced. In terms of the equity coefficient described above, the property tax (0.722) is more regressive than the corporation tax (0.739) or the state sales tax (0.739), but less regressive than the auto license tax (0.626).[f] The under-

---

[f]These equity coefficients are computed net of estimated tax exporting. It is assumed that 20 percent of the local property tax and 60 percent of the state corporation tax are exported and that the state sales tax and the state auto license fees are borne 100 percent by Tennessee residents. The 20 percent exporting figure for the property tax varies as between types of property, e.g., the estimate for industrial property is 94 percent and that for personal property is 16 percent. With respect to the property tax, it is assumed that the exporting percentages derived on a statewide basis will apply as well to metropolitan Nashville.

Table 6-20. Functions Considered for State Government Financial Assumption: Nashville.

Suggested Functions for Shifting	Increase in State Expenditures	Reduction (+) in Metropolitan Nashville Expenditures	Practicality of Shift to State	Methodology Used to Determine Expenditures
Corrections:				
Total shift with no service-level adjustment[a]	$4,717,000	$748,000		Figures used are unadjusted estimates of local cost of corrections in Tennessee for the "confinement and rehabilitation" of suspects and convicted adults and minors.
Total shift at Metro service level	$6,654,000	$748,000	State should administer and finance corrections and jail programs.	Per capita expenditures throughout the state were adjusted to the Metro level.
Total shift with no service-level adjustment plus regional jail plan	$11,717,000	$748,000		Figures consist of unadjusted local expenditures for corrections plus planned $7 million for beginning of construction of regional facilities.
Total shift at Metro service level plus[b] regional jail plan	$13,554,000	$748,000		Projections are of statewide per capita expenditure adjusted at Metro level plus planned construction of regional facilities.
Nonlocal Elections:				
Total shift without service-level adjustment[a,b]	$ 1,528,000	$156,000	State should administer and finance all elections in which state officials are elected. If election is	Figures included are the reported expenditures of county governments on statewide elections in 1970, adjusted to eliminate costs relating to American Party elections.

Table 6-20.(continued)

Suggested Functions for Shifting	Increase in State Expenditures	Reduction (+) in Metropolitan Nashville Expenditures	Practicality of Shift to State	Methodology Used to Determine Expenditures
Nonlocal Elections:			strictly local, the state should administer but the local government should pay the costs.	
Educational—General: Total shift with no service-level adjustment[a]	$184,544,000	$33,179,000	State should increase financing share. Control remain local.	Cost estimates and sources of funds were given by Tennessee Department of Education distributed among grade levels by weighted enrollments derived from the University of Tennessee study's methodology.
Total shift with Metro Service level adjustment[b]	$342,217,000	$33,179,000		Projection of Metro service level throughout state was based on weighted enrollments and Metro expenditure per weighted student.
Education—Special: Total Shift with no service-level adjustment[a]	$4,801,000	$1,261,000	State should assume full finance and administrative responsibility.	Methodology for both parts are identical to section on General Education since this program was considered as part of General Education.
Total shift with Metro service levels[b]	9,359,000	1,261,000		
Education—Transportation: Total shift with no service-level adjustment[a]	$6,928,000	$1,057,000	State should increase financing share. Control	Metro transportation expenditures per nonweighted pupil were projected for entire state.

Table 6-20. (continued)

Suggested Functions for Shifting	Increase in State Expenditures	Reduction (+) in Metropolitan Nashville Expenditures	Practicality of Shift to State	Methodology Used to Determine Expenditures
Education–Transportation: Total shift at Metro service level[b]	8,188,000	1,057,000	remain local.	
Health and Hospitals: Total shift with no service-level adjustment[a]	$94,200,000	$11,323,000		Figures are for current operational and capital expenditures by state and local government with no adjustment: total state funding.
Total shift at Metro service level[b]	$99,200,000	$11,323,000		Total state funding including adjustment to bring all of state to Metro per capita expenditure level without respect to differences in proportions of current costs and capital outlays.
80 percent shift with no service-level adjustment	76,360,000	11,323,000	State should assume complete administrative control and financing responsibilities.	State funding of 80 percent of actual local expenditures as determined in first part, provided that local units continue with a minimum of 20 percent of actual level
80 percent shift with Metro service-level adjustment	79,360,000	11,323,000		State funding of 80 percent of local expenditure after adjustment to Metro level as in second part, providing local units maintain a minimum of 20 percent of Metro per capita expenditure level.

Table 6-20. (continued)

Suggested Functions for Shifting	Increase in State Expenditures	Reduction (+) in Metropolitan Nashville Expenditures	Practicality of Shift to State	Methodology Used to Determine Expenditures
Direct Relief: Total shift with no service-level adjustment[a]	$ 965,000	$387,000		Interviews corroborated by county audits were used to determine expenditures by the four metropolitan counties, coupled with an expenditure approximation derived from the survey for the rest of the state.
Total shift at Metro service level for four Metro areas	1,665,000	387,000	State should assume complete administrative control and financing responsibilities.	Projection includes the adjustment of service level in the four metropolitan counties to the Metropolitan per capita level plus the estimated actual level for the rest of the state.
Total shift at Metro service level[b]	3,395,000	387,000		Projection is of the Metropolitan per capita expenditure for the entire state.
Courts—Net Operating Expenditures: Total shift with no service-level adjustment[a,b]	$1,400,000	−$215,000	State should administer and finance county and municipal courts with local units perhaps retaining traffic and minor violations courts.	Figures are approximations of current costs relating to the administration of state laws at the local level, less the approximated court revenues.

Table 6-20 (continued)

Suggested Functions for Shifting	Increase in State Expenditures	Reduction (+) in Metropolitan Nashville Expenditures	Practicality of Shift to State	Methodology Used to Determine Expenditures
Courts—Net Operating Expenditures:				
Total of shifts with no service-level adjustment[c]	$299,083,000	$47,896,000	State should administer and finance county and municipal courts with local units perhaps retaining traffic and minor violations courts.	Figures are approximations of current costs relating to the administration of state laws at the local level, less the approximated court revenues.
Total of shifts with most expensive service-level adjustment[d]	478,841,000	47,896,000		

[a]Indicates that everything was added to obtain total with no service-level adjustment.
[b]Indicates that everything was added to obtain total with service-level adjustment.
[c]Those included are indicated by superior a (footnote a).
[d]Those included are indicated by superior b (footnote b).

lying assumptions about the incidence of each affected tax are reported in Chapter 5.

Results: The Impact of State Assumption

Three related effects are integral to evaluating the impact of state financial assumption in metropolitan Nashville: (1) changes in the tax burden *distribution;* (2) changes in the tax burden *level;* and (3) changes in the fiscal position of the city government.

Tax Burden Levels. If state assumption is accompanied by significant leveling-up and if the Nashville share of the base of the expanded state tax is high, state financial assumption could result in a marked increase in total tax liabilities of Nashville residents.

As may be seen from Table 6-21, the likely outcome of state financial assumption is a substantial cost increment. For example, from the first row of the table the net cost to Nashville residents of the state's assuming financial responsibility for the corrections function may be estimated. Column 1 shows that if state financial assumption results in no change in the present level of expenditures across the state, total state government expenditures will rise by $4.7 million and Nashville-Davidson municipal expenditures will fall by $748,000. Assuming that this function is financed exclusively from property tax revenues, and taking account of local property tax exporting, the property tax burden of Nashville residents will fall by an estimated $596,000 (column 3).

If the state government uses a sales tax to finance the entire $4.7 million increment, the share to be paid by metropolitan Nashville Residents is $521,000, and therefore Nashville residents will experience a net reduction of $75,000 in total tax payments. If, however, it is assumed that total corrections expenditures will level-up to the Nashville per capita amount in the event of state assumption, the result will be an increment in tax liabilities to Nashville residents of $139,000 (see row 2). This result holds generally for all functions, and as may be seen in the bottom three rows of Table 6-21, if any leveling-up or equalization occurs, substantial increments in resident tax burdens may be expected. For example, if the entire state were to be brought up to the Nashville level of per capita spending for the shifted functions, total resident tax liability would rise by approximately $14 million or $30.14 per person.

Tax Burden Distribution and Level Changes. It might be expected, from the very similar equity coefficients for the taxes to be considered, that the tax burden distribution effects of state assumption will not be great. These effects, described in Table 6-22, show that state assumption, if financed by a sales tax, will tend to heighten the regressivity of the existing system if total expenditures increase because of a leveling-up effect.

Table 6–21. Net Metro Tax Cost or Savings when Functions Are Shifted to the State: 1970.

	Total State Expenditures	Reduction of Metro Expenditure and Property Tax	Local Property Tax Burden	Metro Share of State Sales Tax Burden	Metro Cost of Shift[d]
I. Corrections					
a. Total shift with no service-level adjustment[a]	$ 4,717,000	$ 748,000	$ 596,000	$ 521,000	– $ 75,000
b. Total shift at Metro service level	6,654,000	748,000	596,000	735,000	+139,000
c. Total shift with no service-level adjustment plus regional jail plan	11,717,000	748,000	596,000	1,295,000	+699,000
d. Total shift at Metro service level plus regional jail plan[b]	13,554,000	748,000	596,000	1,498,000	+902,000
II. Nonlocal Elections					
Total shift with service-level adjustment[a,b]	1,528,000	156,000	124,000	169,000	+45,000
III. Educational—General					
a. Total shift with no service-level adjustment[a]	184,544,000	33,179,000	26,417,000	20,392,000	–6,025,000
b. Total shift with Metro service-level adjustment[b]	342,217,000	33,179,000	26,417,000	37,815,000	+11,398,000
IV. Education—Special					
a. Total shift with no service-level adjustment[a]	4,801,000	1,261,000	1,004,000	531,000	–473,000
b. Total shift with Metro service level[b]	9,359,000	1,261,000	1,004,000	1,034,000	+430,000
V. Education—Transportation					
a. Total shift with no service-level adjustment[a]	6,928,000	1,057,000	842,000	766,000	–76,000
b. Total shift at Metro service level[b]	8,188,000	1,057,000	842,000	905,000	+63,000

Table 6-21. (continued)

	Total State Expenditures	Reduction of Metro Expenditure and Property Tax	Local Property Tax Burden	Metro Share of State Sales Tax Burden	Metro Cost of Shift[d]
VI. Health and Hospitals					
a. Total shift with no service-level adjustment[a]	$ 94,200,000	$11,323,000	$ 9,015,000	$10,407,000	+$ 1,392,000
b. Total shift at Metro service level[b]	99,200,000	11,323,000	9,015,000	10,962,000	+1,947,000
c. 80% shift with no service-level adjustment	76,360,000	11,323,000	7,212,000	8,438,000	+1,226,000
d. 80% shift with Metro service-level adjustment	79,360,000	11,323,000	7,212,000	8,769,000	+1,557,000
VII. Direct Relief					
a. Total shift with no service-level adjustment[a]	965,000	387,000	308,000	107,000	−201,000
b. Total shift at Metro service level for four Metro areas	1,665,000	387,000	308,000	184,000	−124,000
c. Total shift at Metro service level[b]	3,395,000	387,000	308,000	375,000	+67,000
VIII. Courts—Net Operating Expenditures					
Total Shift with no service-level adjustment[a,b]	1,400,000	−215,000		155,000	+370,000
IX. Summary of Shifts					
a. Total of shifts with no service-level adjustment	$299,083,000	$47,896,000	$38,091,000	$33,050,000	−$ 5,041,000
b. Total of shifts with all Metro service-level					

Summary of Shifts
adjustments, where
applicable

c. Total of shifts with most
expensive service-level
adjustment

471,941,000	47,896,000	38,091,000	52,150,000	+14,059,000
$478,841,000	$47,896,000	$38,091,000	52,913,000	+$14,822,000

aIndicates that everything was added to obtain total with no service-level adjustment.
bIndicates that everything was added to obtain total with service-level adjustment.
cOnly local property taxes are reduced and only state sales taxes are increased. Figures will vary slightly using other taxes.
dMinus indicates tax savings, plus indicates tax increase.

Table 6-22. Change in Effective Tax Rates Resulting from State Financial Assumption (in cents per dollar of income).[a]

Net Change in Resident Tax Liability[c] (millions of dollars)	General State Sales Taxes[b]			Auto License Fees		
	$3,000-3,999	$9,000-9,999	$25,000+	$3,000-3,999	$9,000-9,999	$25,000+
–$ 5.0	–0.08¢	0.68¢	–0.34¢	–2.47¢	–0.07¢	–0.98¢
14.1	3.06	2.52	–0.77	–0.68	1.36	–0.25
14.8	3.14	2.61	0.80	0.59	1.42	–0.22

[a] Assumes mean class incomes of $3,500, $9,500, and $25,000, respectively.

[b] These results also hold for the corporate income tax.

[c] These three overall tax liability changes correspond to the leveling-up assumptions made. See Table 6-2.

Conclusions

The shifting of financial responsibility for urban functions to the state was not recommended in the Nashville UO report.[13] It was concluded that shifts of local functions to the state government will probably result in increased aggregate taxes for metropolitan Nashville residents and possibly reduced service levels. As shown here, the expected equity gains from state assumption are mild at best. Under present circumstances it would appear that the major gains to be realized from direct state assumption involve administrative efficiencies, the internalizing of statewide externalities, the gaining by the state government of discretionary power over expansion or contraction of heretofore local programs, and increased state government ability to equalize public service levels.

MILWAUKEE[14]

The Milwaukee UO evaluated the fiscal and equity consequences of shifting the financing of education and welfare to the state. In Wisconsin, welfare is a county function and education services are delivered through a set of independent school districts. Hence, neither of these functions results in a drain on the city government budget per se, but both impose a heavy drain on central-city taxpayers. It is estimated that city taxpayers contribute $13.2 million in property taxes to the county, or $18.41 per capita, for support of the welfare function. For education, it is estimated that in 1969-1970 the Milwaukee school district levied $83 million in school property taxes or an amount equivalent to about $117 per capita. If *both* these functions had been shifted to the state government level, then aggregate local property tax payments would have fallen by $92.2 million, or by $134.18 per capita. Whether state financing would have increased or decreased the family tax burden at different income levels is discussed below.

An important methodological departure made in the Milwaukee study is that property taxes on land are assumed to be borne by owners of property; whereas the tax on improvements is assumed to be shifted forward to renters. The allocator used to distribute property taxes paid among income classes is property income earned including imputed rents on owner-occupied property. The nonresidential portion of the property tax is assumed to be passed on to local residents, or exported from the city, in the form of higher prices. The allocator used to distribute total nonexported, nonresidential property taxes among income classes is consumption.

Shifting Education Finance to the State Income Tax

The first model evaluated by the Milwaukee UO was the shifting of local education financing from the local school property tax to the state income tax. Table 6-23 summarizes the position of Milwaukee residents, had such a shift occurred in fiscal 1969-1970. Before shifting, residents and businesses paid

Table 6-23.   Aggregate Tax Liability Effects on Milwaukee Residents of Shifting Education or Welfare Financing to the State Income Tax (millions of dollars).

	Function	
	Education	Welfare
Effects on City Residents:		
Total local property tax financing	$ 83.0	$13.2
Direct property taxes on property owners	44.4	7.2
Indirect property taxes on Milwaukee		
residents	28.2	4.3
Total direct and indirect property		
taxes on Milwaukee residents	72.6	11.5
New Aggregate State Income Taxes		
Necessary	664.2	31.4
Amount of new state income taxes		
obtained from Milwaukee		
residents	112.2	5.3
Aggregate Change in Tax Liability of		
Milwaukee Residents	39.5	−6.2

$83 million for education in fiscal 1969-1970. Of this, $72.6 million was estimated to have been paid by residents. This is the amount by which local taxes on residents would fall if education financing were shifted to the state. If the state assumed all local cost for education, then it would have to raise $664.2 million in new revenues to do so. Assuming the state chose to finance this amount by increasing the state income tax, then Milwaukee residents would have incurred new income tax liabilities totaling $112.1 million. On balance, residents of Milwaukee would have experienced an aggregate tax burden increase of $39.6 million or 44 percent.

As may be seen from Table 6-24, the interpersonal equity effects of shifting education financing from the local property tax to the state income tax are complex. Residents with incomes below $4000 tend to experience tax decreases. Those with incomes about $4000 experience increases. However, the size of the increase is not systematically related to income level.

Shifting Welfare Finance to the State Income Tax

The second function evaluated by the Milwaukee UO is the effect on city residents of shifting welfare financing from the county property tax to the state income tax. Welfare is a county function in Wisconsin, but it is estimated that of the total amount spent on welfare financing by the county, Milwaukee raised $13.2 million. Of this amount, it is estimated that $11.5 million was paid (directly or indirectly) by local residents. This is the amount of

Table 6-24. Changes in Taxes per Dollar of Economic Income Resulting from Shifting Milwaukee's Education Financing from the Local Property Tax to the State Income Tax (in cents per dollar of income).

Income Class	
$0 - 999	−0.50¢
1,000 - 1,999	−2.64
2,000 - 2,999	−1.38
3,000 - 3,999	−0.99
4,000 - 4,999	0.83
5,000 - 5,999	2.06
6,000 - 6,999	1.98
7,000 - 7,999	1.73
8,000 - 8,999	3.41
8,000 - 9,999	2.87
10,000 - 11,999	2.16
12,000 - 14,999	2.71
15,000 - 24,999	1.38
25,000 and over	−1.03

tax reduction that city property owners would have initially experienced had welfare financing been shifted in 1969.

The state, in assuming total financial responsibility for welfare, would have had to raise $31.4 million. As a result, Milwaukee residents would have incurred new tax liabilities of $5.3 million. On balance, then, city residents would have decreased their aggregate tax liabilities by $6.2 million, or 54 percent, or $8.65 per capita (see Table 6-23).

Table 6-25 presents the tax changes per dollar of economic income as a result of shifting welfare financing from the local property tax to the state income tax. With only a couple of exceptions, there is a general pattern among these tax increases. As is shown in Table 6-25, as a family's average income rises, the size of its tax decrease per dollar of economic income tends to decrease. For instance, a family in the $3,000-$3,999 income class tends to experience a tax decrease of 0.4 cents per dollar of economic income. On the other hand, a family in the $12,000-$14,999 income bracket tends to experience a tax decrease of only .09 cents per dollar of economic income.

ATLANTA[15]

The focus of the Atlanta study is on shifting a package of city-financed services to a regional government that is assumed alternatively to encompass a part, or all, of the Atlanta metropolitan area.

Eighteen different services currently provided by the city of Atlanta are considered, and the levels of total expenditures that would have occurred

Table 6-25. Changes in Taxes per Dollar of Economic Income Resulting from Shifting Milwaukee's Portion of Welfare Financing from the Local Property Tax to the State Income Tax (in cents per dollar of income).

Income Class	
$0 - 999	−0.45¢
1,000 - 1,999	−0.22
2,000 - 2,999	−0.43
3,000 - 3,999	−0.44
4,000 - 4,999	−0.34
5,000 - 5,999	−0.22
6,000 - 6,999	−0.20
7,000 - 7,999	−0.18
8,000 - 8,999	−0.10
9,000 - 9,999	−0.10
10,000 - 11,999	−0.10
12,000 - 14,999	−0.09
15,000 - 24,999	−0.16
25,000 and over	−0.42

in 1970—if the service districts had been redefined in four alternative ways[g]—are projected. For eight of the eighteen services, increased expenditures are then projected based on alternative assumptions regarding expenditure increases as a function of some well-defined base. For example, it is projected that $11,659,690 would have been spent on fire protection in 1970 had the fire service district encompassed all of Fulton County. This is based on the assumption that per capita expenditures in Atlanta in 1970 ($19.19) would have remained constant with the increased service-district size. The projection bases and the resulting estimates are summarized in Table 6-26.

Four taxes were considered as alternatives, with rates estimated on the basis of the estimated level of financing required by the various regional governments. The four options considered for regional financing are: (1) a flat percent surtax on the Georgia state income tax rates, or a flat percent local add-on to the state rate; (2) a flat percent local payroll tax; (3) a local percentage add-on to the state sales tax base; and (4) a regional property tax.

After account is taken of tax exporting, the net tax burden of Atlanta residents changes in the following fashion: for all taxes, a shift of expenditures to either Fulton-DeKalb Counties or to the SMSA would result in an increase in the total local tax burden. Only in the case of sales tax financing would expansion to Fulton County yield Atlanta residents any property tax relief, while annexation of the Sandy Springs area would decrease total city tax

---

[g]These four alternative service districts are: Atlanta-Sandy Springs, Fulton County, Fulton and DeKalb Counties, and the five-county SMSA.

Table 6-26. Projected Expenditures.

	Traffic Engineer	Public Works (Other than Sanitation and Administration)	Children & Youth Services Council	Planning	Inspection	City Courts	Community Relations Commission	Fire	Law	Parks, Except Zoo and Cyclorama
Basis for Projected Expenditure	$1,655 mile of road	$6,898 mile of road	$1.35 children under 18	$3,061 square mile	$1.17 per capita	$2.04 per capita	12¢ per capita	$19.19 per capita	$1.03 per capita	$9.16 per capita
Atlanta Net Expenditures from general funds	$2,257,352	$8,394.267	$115,231	$416,253	$551,341	$961,320	$58,724	$9,018,139	$484,577	$4,306,628
Projected expenditures as a % of Atlanta expenditures	100%	100%	100%	100%	100%	100%	100%	100%	100%	100%
Atlanta-Sandy Springs projected expenditures	$2,543,022	$9,456,559	$120,943	$553,385	$581,669	$1,014,199	$61,835	$9,515,563	$511,276	$4,544,072
Projected expenditures as a % of original Atlanta expenditures	113%	113%	105%	133%	106%	106%	105%	106%	106%	106%
Fulton Projected expenditures	$4,778,480	$17,769,248	$141,992	$1,622,330	$710,883	$1,239,488	$72,911	$11,659,690	$625,820	$5,565,543

(continued)

Table 6-26. (continued)

	Traffic Engineer	Public Works (Other than Sanitation and Administration)	Children & Youth Services Council	Planning	Inspection	City Courts	Community Relation Commission	Fire	Law	Parks, Except Zoo and Cyclorama
Projected expenditures as a % of Atlanta expenditures	212%	212%	123%	390%	129%	129%	124%	129%	129%	129%
Fulton-DeKalb										
Projected expenditures	$7,811,405	$29,047,478	$250,352	$4,548,646	$1,196,886	$2,086,877	$122,757	$19,630,967	$1,053,669	$ 9,370,488
Projected expenditures as a % of Atlanta expenditures	344%	344%	217%	1111%	217%	217%	217%	217%	217%	217%
SMSA										
Projected expenditures	$13,829,025	$51,424,590	$351,141	$7,361,705	$1,626,492	$2,836,147	$166,819	$26,677,247	$1,431,869	$12,733,903
Projected expenditures as a % of Atlanta expenditures	613%	613%	305%	1769%	295%	295%	284%	296%	295%	296%

burdens if either a sales or payroll tax were levied. Interestingly, in no case would use of a local income tax provide property tax relief. Further, if the state would insist upon usage of property taxes, no net financial gain would be experienced by Atlanta residents if other service districts were created. These changes are described in Table 6-27.

The interpersonal equity effects of reassignment of these functions to an SMSA financing district are described in Table 6-28. While Table 6-27 indicated that in only three of the twenty combinations of service districts and financing schemes would Atlantans receive net tax relief, there would likely be some gainers in Atlanta in each combination, except when the property tax is used. Since all property tax burdens increase no matter what the service district definition, any service-district expanation using property tax financing would result in increased local taxes for all income groups. While either form of income tax would result in increased total local tax burdens for all service districts, the progressive nature of the income tax would result in tax savings for low-income families.

The payroll and sales tax levies show more varied results. Lower income groups gain under the payroll tax, and the lowest income group loses under the sales tax. The direction and amount of change in tax burdens for the higher income groups depend both upon the service-district definition and whether a sales or payroll tax is used. So creation of a metropolitan financing district would increase tax burdens of higher income groups more under a sales tax than under a payroll tax, with the over-$10,000 group being hardest hit.

NOTES

1. Katherine Bradbury, Philip Moss, and Joseph S. Slavet, *Reallocation of Selected Municipal Services to the State: A Municipal Finance Alternative,* (Boston, Mass.: The Boston Urgan Observatory, October 1973).
2. Bureau of Public Affairs, *Impact of the State-Local Tax Services Mix on Municipal Finances in the Boston Metropolitan Area: A Preliminary Evaluation* (Boston, Mass.: The Boston Urban Observatory, 1972).
3. K. Hubbell, J. Olson, S. Ramenossky, and J. Ward, *Alternative Methods for Financing Public Services: The Cases of Education and Welfare, Kansas City, Missouri* (Kansas City, Mo.: Kansas City Urban Observatory, August 1973).
4. A good analysis of the Kansas City metropolitan area fisc is given in L. Kenneth Hubbell and G. Ross Stephens, *Local Finance and Revenue-Sharing in the Kansas City SMSA, 1957 to 1980* (Kansas City, Mo.: Mid-America Urban Observatory, August 1972.
5. George Babilot, W.R. Bigger, and James D. Kitchen, *Shifting Public Functions and the Distribution of Tax Burden by Economic Class: A Model and Empirical Observation* (San Diego: San Diego Urban Observatory, June 1972).

Table 6-27. Changes in Net Tax Burden[a] of Atlanta Residents When Service Package is Shifted to Alternative Regional Governments.

Area	Surtax	Income	Payroll	Sales	Property
Atlanta	$11,842,854	$11,842,854	−$ 2,255,782[b]	−$ 6,767,346[b]	$ 0
Atlanta Sandy Springs	10,643,870	11,257,468	− 1,321,280	− 5,999,961	212,713
Fulton	15,071,309	17,885,553	− 6,159,536	876,075	8,035,698
Fulton DeKalb	18,730,920	20,325,708	− 11,554,374	5,972,615	12,351,768
SMSA	26,391,401	27,648,631	− 23,876,941	13,819,102	20,105,251

[a]Net = [Atlanta residents nonexported share of regional expenditure after shifting] − [Atlanta's expenditure on these functions from local sources not exported].

[b]Minus symbol means decrease in tax burdens.

Table 6-28. Net Change in Taxes When Financing of the Service Package is Shifted to Alternative Regional Taxes (in cents per dollar of income).

Income Class	Surtax	Income Tax Add-on	Payroll	Sales	Property
$0 - 999	-1.98¢	-1.98¢	-1.56¢	4.89¢	2.43¢
1,000 - 1,999	-0.71	-0.71	-0.02	2.88	0.44
2,000 - 2,999	-0.56	-0.56	-0.17	1.81	0.69
3,000 - 3,999	-0.81	-0.81	-0.16	1.03	1.00
4,000 - 4,999	-0.93	-0.80	-0.05	0.45	1.20
5,000 - 5,999	-0.85	-0.52	0.14	0.30	1.28
6,000 - 6,999	-0.70	-0.23	0.44	0.31	1.30
7,000 - 7,999	-0.43	0.15	0.79	0.40	1.20
8,000 - 8,999	-0.25	0.52	1.08	0.40	1.38
9,000 - 9,999	-0.17	0.71	0.92	0.39	1.27
10,000 - 11,999	0.39	1.07	1.13	5.74	1.14
12,000 - 14,999	1.03	1.52	1.41	7.29	0.85
15,000 - 24,999	1.50	1.62	1.44	7.28	0.77
25,000 and over	2.55	1.76	0.86	3.64	0.76

6. George Babilot, W.R. Bigger, and James D. Kitchen, *A Study of Local Government Finance in the San Diego SMSA* (San Diego: San Diego Urban Observatory, June 1972).

7. William Oakland and Eliyahu Borukhov, *Incidence and Other Fiscal Impacts of the Reform of Educational Finance: A Case Study of Baltimore* (Baltimore: Baltimore Urban Observatory, April 1974).

8. William Oakland, Eliyahu Borukhov, Frederick T. Sparrow, and Albert Teplin, *Baltimore Municipal Finance Study* (Baltimore: Baltimore Urban Observatory, July 1972).

9. William Winter, Cris Tomasides, James Adams, and John Richeson, *Local Government Finance in the Denver Metropolitan Area, First Year Report* (Denver: Denver Urban Observatory, April 1972).

10. William Winter, Cris Tomasides, James Adams, and John Richeson, *Local Government Finance in the Denver Metropolitan Area, Second Year Report* (Denver: Denver Urban Observatory, November 1973).

11. William Perry, Robert Horton and J. Edmund Newman, *The Impact of State Assumption of Selected Metropolitan Nashville Expenditure Programs* (Nashville: Urban Observatory of Metropolitan Nashville, February 1974).

12. James D. Evans, *Expenditure and Revenue Analysis: 1956-1971 for Metropolitan Nashville-Davidson County* (Nashville: Office of the Mayor, 1973).

13. Perry, Horton, and Newman, op. cit.

14. Arthur P. Becker, "Property Tax Reform: An Analysis of a Proposal for Milwaukee," *Proceedings of the Sixty Seventh Annual Conference 1974*, National Tax Association—Tax Institute of America, pp. 93–128; and Arthur P. Becker and Hans Robert Isakson, "The Burden on the City of Milwaukee and Its Residents of the Real Property Tax Compared with the Income Tax," unpublished manuscript presented at the Thirteenth Annual Conference of the Committee on Taxation, Resources and Economic Development, Madison, Wisconsin, October 25-27, 1974.

15. David L. Sjoquist, Larry D. Schroeder, and William H. Wilken, *Shifting Public Service Functions: Expenditure-Revenue Effects and Political Feasibility*, (Atlanta, Georgia: Atlanta Urban Observatory, April 1974).

Chapter Seven

A Comparison of Tax Burden Effects

The central-city functions discussed as candidates for financial reassignment to the state or regional government may be divided into education, welfare, and a residual group we refer to as the service package. In this chapter we develop an intercity comparison of the tax burden impact of each of these shifts, first on the aggregate tax liability of central-city residents, and then on the distribution of tax burdens among families in different income classes. In doing this we consider the implications of each reform on the budget position of the central-city government.

The tax burden effects observed in these case analyses are attributable to all of (1) increased service levels; (2) a shifting of relative tax payments from one area of the state/region to another; and (3) a change in the relative size of effective tax rates in different income classes. Since all of these changes are likely to accompany state or regional financial assumption, all are considered here.

EDUCATION

The effects of state government assumption of education finance on the aggregate tax liability of central-city residents, summarized in Table 7-1, vary widely among the UO cities studied. These results suggest that the overall tax liability of central-city residents will rise under state financial assumption. This result appears to hold under differing assumptions about the state tax used or the amount of leveling-up assumed to occur. The size of this increased tax liability is striking—over 50 percent in Baltimore if the state sales tax is the means of finance, over 40 percent in Milwaukee if the state income tax is used, and over 60 percent in San Diego if a combination of state sales and income taxes is used (see Table 7-1). Therefore, the model applied here produces some hard evidence that state assumption of education finance would increase the aggregate tax liabilities of central-city residents.

Table 7-1. Change in Aggregate City Resident Tax Liabilities Resulting from State Government Assumption of Education Financing.

	State Sales Tax		State Income Tax		State Sales and Income Tax	State Residential Property and Income Tax[a]	
	Baltimore[b]	Nashville-Davidson[c]	Baltimore[b]	Milwaukee[c]	San Diego[c]	Kansas City, Missouri	Kansas City, Kansas
Aggregate Tax Liability of City Residents[d] (millions of dollars)							
Before State Assumption	$36.4	$26.4	$36.4	$ 72.6	$44.7	$15.9	$ 3.0
After State Assumption	61.2	20.3	52.3	112.2	65.5	20.9	5.2
Change	$24.8	–$ 6.1	$15.9	$39.6	$20.8	$ 5.0	$ 2.2
Per Capita Tax Liability (in dollars)							
Before State Assumption	$40.19	$61.96	$40.19	$101.20	$57.60	$31.35	$17.83
After State Assumption	67.50	47.64	57.70	156.48	94.00	41.20	30.90
Per Capita Change	$27.31	–$14.32	$16.51	$44.28	$36.40	$ 9.85	$13.07
Percent Change	67.90%	23.10%	41.10%	43.80%	63.20%	31.40%	73.30%
Effect on Locally Raised Revenues for City Government Budget (millions of dollars)	–$76.6	–$33.2	–$76.6	–$83.0	–$52.7	–$15.9	–$ 3.0
Locally Financed Education Expenditures as a Percent of Total Revenues from Local Sources[e]	29.0%	26.0%	29.0%	47.5%	42.1%	15.4%	15.2%

[a] Described as Proposal 2 in Chapter 6, and assumes full equalization of expenditures per ADA at $650–a 10 percent increment over the current level.
[b] Assumes an equalized statewide per pupil expenditure at $957, as compared with the current level of $938.
[c] Expenditures are assumed to continue at current levels.
[d] The tax liability of city residents differs from the amount of taxes raised for education by the amount of tax exported to nonresidents. For example, locally raised taxes for education in Baltimore are $76.6 million, while $36.4 million of this was paid by Baltimore residents. This means that $40.2 million of locally raised revenues for education were exported to nonresidents.
[e] City taxes raised locally in this case denotes revenues raised locally for all city government functions, including education.

There are two factors operating that cause this effect, which amounts to city residents financing a larger share of statewide expenditures than they presently do. One is the shifting of taxes away from a combination of business and individual taxes (that is, the local property tax) toward taxes strictly on individuals (such as individual income and retail sales taxes). While under the local property tax, residents in the city pay only a fraction of their education bill, under state government taxes the possibilities for exporting are substantially reduced or eliminated. So, a replacement of local property taxes with equal-yield state taxes would increase city resident tax liabilities, with the increase being greater if the city has a greater concentration of export-type industry than does the rest of the state. This explains the particularly high increases observed for Baltimore and Milwaukee.

The second effect has to do with intrastate disparities in the level of education expenditures. If education expenditures in the city are relatively lower than those in the rest of the state (a common pattern for central cities), then it is likely that the city's share of state taxes to finance total education expenditures will, in amount, exceed its previous level of locally raised education expenditures. In this respect, note from Table 7-1 that Nashville-Davidson is the only city that has higher per capita expenditures from local sources than other local governments in the state, and that only Nashville-Davidson shows a decline in the aggregate tax liabilities as a result of state government financial assumption.

Though aggregate tax liabilities in these cities generally rise as a result of direct state assumption of education finance, it does not necessarily follow that families in all income brackets experience tax burden increases. The data in Table 7-2 show the change in tax payments per dollar of income that results from state government assumption of education finance. For example, if the state of Maryland assumes total financial responsibility for the education function, and finances its increased expenditures with an income tax, a Baltimore family with an income between $3,000 and $3,999 would experience a tax reduction of 1.45 cents per dollar of income. If this family's income were $3,500, its total annual tax reduction would be $50.75.

In general these results show that state assumption tends to result in tax increases for family units in the higher income classes, particularly when personal income tax financing is used. Yet even this generalization requires qualifications, for the results vary considerably among cities. Most of the variation appears to be due to the choice of the state tax to be used, and to the structure of the state tax. In this respect five of the six cities proposed consideration of both, or a mix of, state income and sales taxes. The general consensus was that sole use of the sales or income tax would require rate increases that would be difficult to obtain. The mixing of two state taxes avoids the high rates necessary if only one tax is used.

There is a dramatic difference in results between Baltimore and Nashville-Davidson, even in the case where both would finance education expenditures with the state sales tax. In Baltimore, those below the $5,000 income

Table 7-2. Changes in Taxes Per Dollar of Economic Income Resulting from State Government Assumption of Education Finance (in cents per dollar of income).

Income Class	State Sales Tax		State Personal Income Tax		State Sales and Personal Income Tax	State Residential Property and State Personal Income Tax	
	Baltimore	Nashville-Davidson[a]	Baltimore	Milwaukee	San Diego	Kansas City, Missouri	Kansas City, Kansas
$0 - 999	-1.33¢	2.35¢	-4.00¢	-0.50¢	-5.9¢	-8.15¢	-4.56¢
1,000 - 1,999	-1.33	.06	-4.00	-2.64	-3.4	-2.11	-0.88
2,000 - 2,999	-1.33	.05	-4.00	-1.38	-2.6	-1.48	-0.73
3,000 - 3,999	0.29	-1.15	-1.45	-0.99	-2.1	-1.13	-0.61
4,000 - 4,999	0.29	-0.78	-1.45	0.83	-1.6	-0.88	-0.58
5,000 - 5,999	0.33	-0.63	-1.02	2.06	-1.1	-0.68	-0.25
6,000 - 6,999	0.33	-0.58	-1.02	1.98	-0.8	-0.54	0.04
7,000 - 7,999	0.31	-0.39	-0.19	1.73	-0.5	-0.31	0.21
8,000 - 8,999	0.31	-0.37	-0.19	3.41	-0.3	-0.21	0.37
9,000 - 9,999	0.31	-0.31	-0.19	2.87	-0.3	-0.09	0.46
10,000 - 11,999	0.32	-0.30	0.39	2.16	-0.2	0.11	0.25
12,000 - 14,999	0.32	-0.23	0.39	2.71	0.1	0.13	0.35
15,000 - 24,999	0.29	-0.18	0.84	1.38	0.6	0.38	0.11
25,000 and over	0.79	-0.16	1.18	-1.03	1.5	0.43	0.78
					-2.1		

[a]The full range of estimates for each function was not reported in the Nashville study. These are our estimates based on their assumptions and available data.

level experience tax decreases, while residents of Nashville-Davidson with incomes below $3,000 experience tax increases. This effect is a reflection of the differences in the sales tax base used in Maryland and Tennessee. In Tennessee, food purchases are not exempt as they are in Maryland. Because food expenditures account for approximately 25 percent of total expenditures made by low-income families, the results simply reflect the greater regressivity of the sales tax in Tennessee than in Maryland. Although this comparison of the interpersonal equity effects is for only two cities, it does serve to illustrate that state financial assumption via state sales taxation can produce very different effects on interpersonal equity.

In general, however, there is a consistency in the conclusions reached. The results presented in Table 7-2 indicate that state assumption of education financing generally results in tax decreases for lower income families and tax increases for higher income families. Moreover, the tax decreases are inversely related to income, while the tax increases rise as income rises: the poorer a family, the greater the tax relief; and the richer, the greater the tax increment. San Diego stands out among this group in that its proposed financial centralization program would afford the greatest tax relief to families with low incomes (below $7,000), and impose the largest tax increases per income class of any city to families with incomes above $12,000. So in San Diego this type of centralization would do more to redistribute income through the tax structure than in any other city considering this shift.

The two main conclusions to be drawn from these case studies of state assumption of education finance are:

1. The aggregate tax burden on central-city residents will probably increase, particularly in cities where central-city/outside-central-city disparities are great, the concentration of exporting industries in the central city is heavy, and where substantial statewide leveling-up will be required. In such cases, resident tax liabilities could increase by as much as 50 percent.
2. Even with these increases in aggregate tax liability, the tax burdens of lower income city families declines and that for higher income city families rises. The degree of this heightened progressivity of tax burdens depends on the state government tax that is used. Because of the increase in aggregate tax liability on city residents, the city government is not likely to experience substantial budgetary relief; that is, resources will not be freed-up for other uses.

WELFARE

Two cities—Milwaukee[a] and Denver—considered the impact of centralization of welfare financing. In both cases a complete transfer to state government finan-

---

[a]In Wisconsin, welfare is a county responsibility. The amounts referred to as Milwaukee welfare expenditures are estimates of their share of the county welfare expenditures.

cing was proposed. Milwaukee proposed shifting local welfare financing from the county property tax to the state income tax. This shift would require that state income tax rates be increased by 7 percent. Denver also proposed shifting from a city property tax to a state income tax. This would require that a state income tax surcharge of 25 percent be levied. There is no leveling-up issue involved, and the results turn simply on the effective rate patterns of the taxes involved and on the relative ability of the two central cities to export the local property tax. If the shift is to a state personal income tax, as proposed here, Milwaukee residents would *decrease* their average per capita tax liabilities for welfare by 53.9 percent (over $8 per capita), while the decrease for Denver is 11.4 percent (over $1 per capita; see Table 7-3).

Setting aside for the moment these per capita differences, one conclusion is clear: the aggregate tax liability of central-city residents is lower after state assumption. This results for exactly the opposite reason that city resident tax liabilities for education are higher after state assumption: central-city expenditures on welfare from local sources are higher than in the rest of the state, whereas for education they are lower. Because of this, after centralization residents in the balance of the state pay some portion of the central city's welfare cost.

The interpersonal equity effects of centralization of welfare financing, shown in Table 7-4, are similar in the two cities in that most residents experience tax decreases. But the patterns vary. In Milwaukee the tax burdens in all income classes are reduced, that is, the shift to a more progressive state tax is more than offset—even in the highest income classes—by the net shift of total statewide welfare costs from Milwaukee to other local governments in the state. It may also be noted here that there is no monotonic relationship between tax burden changes and family income level. This results in part because of the different property tax incidence assumptions in the Milwaukee study.

The results for Denver show that tax burdens decline below an income level of $15,000, but rise thereafter due to the traditional property tax incidence assumption used in the Denver study and to the structure of the Colorado income tax. These results for Denver show that even in the face of a reduction in aggregate tax liability for welfare, central-city families in the higher income classes could realize tax increases.

The conclusions to be drawn from these two case studies of the impact of state assumption of welfare financing are:

1. Central city residents, in aggregate, will experience tax relief.
2. The central-city government could receive budget relief since local property tax relief could be used for either tax reductions and/or could be applied to other functions.
3. Most central-city residents will experience decreases in effective tax rates depending on the state tax used, and the equity of the effective rate pattern will be improved, particularly if the state income tax is used.

Table 7-3. Change in Aggregate City Resident Tax Liabilities Resulting from State Government Assumption of Welfare Financing.

	Personal Income Tax	
	Milwaukee	*Denver*
Aggregate Tax Liability of City Residents (millions of dollars)		
Before State Assumption	$11.5	$ 6.1
After State Assumption	5.3	5.4
Change	−$ 6.2	−$ 0.7
Per Capita Tax Liability (in dollars)		
Before State Assumption	$16.03	$11.85
After State Assumption	7.39	10.49
Per Capita Change	−8.64	−1.36
Percent Change	−53.90%	−11.40%
Effect on Locally Raised Revenues for City Government Budget (millions of dollars)	−$13.2	−$ 7.5
Locally, Raised Welfare Expenditure as a Percent of Total Revenue Raised from Local Sources	12.6%	6.8%

Table 7-4. Changes in Taxes Per Dollar of Economic Income Resulting from State Government Assumption of Welfare Financing (in cents per dollar of income).

Income Class	Personal Income Tax	
	Milwaukee	*Denver*
$0 - 999	−0.44¢	−14.02¢
1,000 - 1,999	−0.22	−0.51
2,000 - 2,999	−0.43	−0.40
3,000 - 3,999	−0.44	−0.31
4,000 - 4,999	−0.34	−0.31
5,000 - 5,999	−0.22	−0.23
6,000 - 6,999	−0.20	−0.18
7,000 - 7,999	−0.18	−0.17
8,000 - 8,999	−0.10	−0.15
8,000 - 9,999	−0.10	−0.11
10,000 - 11,999	−0.10	−0.12
12,000 - 14,999	−0.10	−0.12
14,000 - 24,999	−0.16	0.22
25,000 and over	−0.42	0.08

THE SERVICE PACKAGE

Lumped together as the service package are a variety of public functions and subfunctions. Their inclusion here as a group enables us to estimate the impact of financial centralization of a smaller group of subfunctions thought to be feasible candidates for financial centralization. While the larger and seemingly more troublesome functions—education and welfare—receive the bulk of reform attention, there is a wide range of local government activities that, if removed from city government budgets, could bring marked fiscal relief.

The shifting of the service package to a higher government level is complicated by the fact that two different "higher" levels of government are considered as the receiving government. In San Diego, Atlanta, and Denver, a regional financing district is proposed as the receiving government. On the other hand, Boston considered shifting the service package to the state government.[b] The results of these programs on aggregate central-city tax liabilities are summarized in Table 7-5.

Expenditure for the proposed service package to be shifted represents approximately 28 percent of locally raised revenues in Boston and Atlanta, but only between 7 and 8 percent in San Diego and Denver. In any of the cities studied, shifting of the service package would, theoretically, free up some locally raised revenues, and assuming that the freed-up revenues are used to grant tax relief, the effects on the aggregate tax liabilities of city residents vary from slight to sizable. Generally, in per capita terms, there is tax *relief* experienced by central-city residents in San Diego and Denver (if the shift is to a regional property or sales tax), but it is not substantial. However, in the Atlanta case the result is an increase in aggregate tax liabilities, primarily because of leveling-up effects. In Boston there would appear to be significant budget relief. The shift to a package of income, sales, and motor fuel taxes in Boston would lower per capita tax liabilities (for support of these functions) to half their previous levels. The implications here are clear. The shifting of the service package to either regional or state government allows Boston central-city residents to shift a portion of the cost of providing urban public services on to residents outside of the city.

The interpersonal equity effects of centralization are shown in Table 7-6. In general the results are consistent in implying tax decreases for most or all families.

Denver and Altanta evaluated the interpersonal equity effects due to a shift from the city property tax to a regional sales tax. The results of this type of centralization are similar, in that lower income family units experience tax increases. But in the Denver case these tax increases turn to decreases at a relatively low level of family income, while in Atlanta all income classes ex-

---

[b]In addition, a package of noneducation functions was proposed for shifting to the state in the Nashville study, but it was not possible to separate these from the education function for purposes here.

Table 7-5. Change in Aggregate City Resident Tax Liabilities Resulting from State and Regional Government Assumption of the Service Package.

	Regional Property Tax			Regional Sales Tax		State, Sales, Motor Fuel, and Income Tax
	San Diego	Atlanta[a]	Denver	Denver	Atlanta	Boston
Aggregate Tax Liability of City Residents (millions of dollars)						
Before Centralization	$ 3.9	$ 16.4	$ 7.0	$ 7.0	$16.4	$47.0
After Centralization	1.5	36.5	3.6	3.8	30.2	23.1
Change	–$ 2.4	$ 20.1	–$ 3.4	–$ 3.2	$13.8	–$23.9
Per Capita Tax Liability (in dollars)						
Before Centralization	$ 5.60	$ 33.00	$13.60	$13.60	$33.00	$94.57
After Centralization	2.15	73.45	6.90	7.38	60.77	46.48
Per Capita Change	–$ 3.45	$ 40.45	–$ 6.70	–$ 6.22	$27.77	–$48.09
Percent Change	– 61.50%	122.60%	–49.20%	–45.70%	–84.10%	–50.80%
Effect on Locally Raised Revenues for City Government Budget (millions of dollars)	$ 4.6	$ 23.7	$ 8.7	$ 8.7	$23.7	$73.8
Locally Raised Financing of the Service Package as a Percent of Total Revenues from Local Sources[b]	7.0%	28.3%	7.9%	7.9%	28.3%	27.0%

[a]Assuming the creation of a metropolitan areawide government.
[b]City budget in this case denotes only revenues raised for local noneducational expenditures. However, cities with dependent school districts include education revenues raised locally.

Table 7-6. Changes in Taxes per Dollar of Economic Income Resulting from State and Regional Government Assumption of the Service Package (in cents per dollar of income).

Income Class	Regional Property Tax			Regional Sales Tax		Personal Income, Sales and Motor Fuel Tax
	San Diego	Atlanta	Denver	Denver	Atlanta	Boston
$0 - 999	-0.20¢	2.43¢	-5.20¢	1.30¢	4.89¢	n/a
1,000 - 1,999	-0.12	0.44	-0.19	0.08	2.88	-5.26¢
2,000 - 2,999	-0.09	0.69	-0.15	0.09	1.81	-3.76
3,000 - 3,999	-0.07	1.00	-0.12	0.01	1.03	-2.66
4,000 - 4,999	-0.07	1.20	-0.13	0.01	0.45	-2.07
5,000 - 5,999	-0.07	1.28	-0.11	0.00	0.30	-1.80
6,000 - 6,999	-0.06	1.30	-0.10	-0.01	0.31	-1.52
7,000 - 7,999	-0.06	1.20	-0.10	-0.01	0.40	-1.16
8,000 - 8,999	-0.06	1.38	-0.10	-0.06	0.40	-1.03
9,000 - 9,999	-0.06	1.27	-0.10	-0.05	0.39	-0.92
10,000 - 11,999	-0.05	1.14	-0.12	-0.13	5.74	-0.76
12,000 - 14,999	-0.05	0.85	-0.12	-0.16	7.29	-0.65
15,000 - 24,999	-0.04	0.77	-0.11	-0.17	7.28	-0.43
25,000 and over	-0.03	0.76	-0.04	-0.05	3.64	-0.29

perience tax increases. Similar results are observed when the shift is to a regional property tax, though it should be emphasized that the tax burden changes are marginal in the San Diego and Denver cases because the expenditure amounts involved are very small.

The Boston study considers a shift of the service package to a combination of state taxes. Two alternatives considered were shifting the service package to a combination of either the state income and motor fuel tax, or to a combination of state income, motor fuel, and sales taxes. The interpersonal equity effects are similar for the two alternatives in that both result in tax decreases throughout most of the income distribution, but the second alternative results in smaller tax decreases up to the $7,000 income level and in general would appear not to heighten the progressivity of the system as much as the first.

Of the three alternatives shown in Tables 7-5 and 7-6, two have similar effects. Shifting to a regional property tax (an alternative suggested for San Diego, Denver, and Atlanta) produces results similar to a shift to state sales, income, and motor fuel tax (an alternative suggested for Boston). Both alternatives result in tax decreases for the lowest income groups. The alternative of shifting financing of the service package to a regional sales tax had distributional effects (the alternative evaluated by Atlanta and Denver) that are quite different from the other three alternatives, that is, tax *increases* in the lower income classes. Again, the Atlanta results are heavily influenced by the expenditure leveling-up effects.

The general conclusions to be drawn from these case studies are that:

1. The amount of budget relief to be gained by central-city governments when the service package is shifted varies widely, and is not always substantial.
2. In aggregate, the tax liabilities of central-city residents decrease.
3. Lower income central-city residents may experience tax decreases, but since sales and income taxes are generally proposed for regional shifts, their burden declines may be only slight, or they may experience tax increases.

THE TOTAL PACKAGE

If the reforms proposed here were undertaken in all nine cities, it would indeed be a sweeping change in intergovernmental financing arrangements in these nine states. Assuming for the moment that such a change were politically feasible, the pattern of tax burden distribution both among jurisdictions within the state and among families in different income classes would be markedly altered. There would, as well, be a substantial relief of pressures on the core-city budget. In short, state assumption would improve interjurisdictional and interpersonal equity in tax burdens, and might tend to equalize service levels, but it would probably raise overall tax burdens on central-city residents.

To quantitatively demonstrate these effects, assume that *all* functional reassignments proposed above are carried out. In such a case the effects in question are: (1) changes in the short-term budgetary position of the city government; (2) changes in the aggregate tax liabilities of central-city residents; (3) changes in the distribution of effective tax rates across income classes within the city; and (4) changes in the *level* of tax payments by families in different income classes.

These effects are clear, and are summarized in Tables 7-7 and 7-8. With respect to city budget relief, the amount of resources freed-up by fiscal centralization are substantial. They range from a high of over 50 percent of all locally raised revenues in Milwaukee and San Diego, to a low of about 15 percent in Denver. At least three things may happen to these freed-up resources: (1) they may go to pay increased state/regional taxes to finance the shifted functions; (2) they may be diverted to other central-city government uses; or (3) they may be returned to residents (businesses) in the form of tax relief. Obviously, the second alternative has the most favorable effect on the budgetary problem facing the city government. But even if city governments are not able to augment tax resources because of functional reassignment, there clearly will be long-term budget relief. The shifting of costly functions (such as education and welfare) to a higher level of government brings about a better balance between the growth in expenditure requirements and the growth in the local property tax base, and leaves the city in a position of being better able to cope financially with the problems of providing services to the poor.

As noted above, while the city budget may be relieved by financial centralization, the aggregate tax liability of central-city residents may actually rise. This effect depends on a number of factors that might be generally summarized as follows: *cet. par.,* the aggregate tax liability to central-city residents will be pushed upward if (1) greater leveling-up will result; (2) state or regional income taxes are *not* used; (3) the central city has a heavy concentration of export-type industries; and (4) the central-city share of *total* state/regional spending on the proposed functions is high. For example, an increase in resident liability would certainly be expected in Baltimore's proposed shift of education finance to the state, where conditions 1, 2, and 3 are present. Note, in this connection, that Baltimore, Milwaukee, and San Diego all experience major resident tax liability increases that can be explained by some combination of these factors. Similar reasoning can be used to explain the relatively large reduction in aggregate taxpayer liabilities in Boston and Nashville; for instance Boston's expenditures on the package of functions proposed for shifting is a relatively small proportion of the statewide total, and an income tax is included in the proposed financing mix. Finally, in all cities it would appear that financial centralization results in a marked improvement in the distribution of tax burdens (see Table 7-8). In some cases—Milwaukee, San Diego, Boston, Baltimore— the size of the tax burden reduction in the lower income classes is a substantial 1 to 3 percent of income. However, from these results one may not say that the

Table 7-7. Change in Aggregate City Resident Tax Liabilities Resulting from State and Regional Government Financial Assumption.

	Atlanta	Baltimore	Boston	Denver	Milwaukee	Kansas City, Kansas	Kansas City, Missouri	Nashville-Davidson	San Diego
Aggregate Tax Liability of City Residents (millions of dollars)									
Before Centralization	$16.4	$36.4	$47.0	$13.1	$100.0	$ 3.0	$15.9	$26.4	$48.6
After Centralization	30.2	52.3	27.6	9.0	131.0	5.2	20.9	20.3	67.0
Change	$13.8	$15.9	–$19.4	–$ 4.1	$ 31.0	$ 2.2	$ 5.0	–$ 6.1	$18.4
Per Capita Tax Liability (in dollars)									
Before Centralization	$33.00	$40.19	$94.57	$25.45	$139.40	$17.83	$31.35	$61.96	$63.20
After Centralization	60.77	57.70	46.48	17.39	182.60	30.90	41.20	47.64	96.15
Change	$27.77	$16.51	–$48.09	$ 8.06	$ 43.20	$13.07	$ 9.85	–$14.32	$32.95
Percent Change	84.10%	41.10%	–50.80%	31.70%	30.99%	73.30%	31.40%	23.10%	52.10%
Reduction in Locally Raised Revenues for City Government Budget (in millions of dollars)	$23.7	$76.6	$73.8	$16.2	$114.2	$ 3.0	$15.9	$33.2	$57.4
Locally Raised Revenues for the Functions Centralized as a Percent of Total Locally Raised Revenues	28.3%	29.0%[a]	27.0%	14.7%	61.1%[a,b]	15.2%[a]	15.4%[a]	26.0%[a]	45.9%[a]

[a]Revenues raised locally for all functions including education.
[b]Including revenues raised by county from Milwaukee residents for education.

Table 7-8. Changes in Taxes per Dollar of Economic Income Resulting from State and Regional Assumption of City Government Functions (in cents per dollar of income)

Income Class	Milwaukee	Denver	San Diego	Boston	Kansas City, Kansas	Kansas City, Missouri	Nashville-Davidson	Baltimore	Atlanta
$0 - 999	-0.94¢	-19.22¢	-6.10¢	n/a	-4.56¢	-8.15¢	2.35¢	-4.00¢	4.89¢
1,000 - 1,999	-2.86	- 0.70	-3.52	-5.36¢	-0.88	-2.11	0.06	-4.00	2.88
2,000 - 2,999	-1.81	- 0.55	-2.69	-3.76	-0.73	-1.48	0.05	-4.00	1.81
3,000 - 3,999	-1.43	- 0.33	-2.17	-2.66	-0.61	-1.13	-1.15	-1.45	1.03
4,000 - 4,999	1.17	- 0.44	-1.67	-2.07	-0.58	-0.88	-0.78	-1.45	0.45
5,000 - 5,999	1.84	- 0.34	-1.17	-1.80	-0.25	-0.68	-0.63	-1.02	0.30
6,000 - 6,999	1.78	- 0.28	-0.86	-1.57	0.04	-0.54	-0.58	-1.02	0.31
7,000 - 7,999	1.55	- 0.27	-0.56	-1.16	0.21	-0.31	-0.39	-0.19	0.40
8,000 - 8,999	3.31	- 0.25	-0.36	-1.03	0.37	-0.21	-0.37	-0.19	0.40
9,000 - 9,999	2.77	- 0.21	-0.26	-0.92	0.46	-0.09	-0.31	-0.19	0.39
10,000 - 11,999	2.06	- 0.24	0.95	-0.76	0.25	0.11	-0.30	0.39	5.74
12,000 - 14,999	2.61	- 0.24	0.55	-0.65	0.35	0.13	-0.23	0.39	7.29
15,000 - 24,999	1.22	0.11	1.46	-0.47	0.11	0.38	-0.18	0.84	7.28
25,000 and over	-1.45	0.04	-2.13	-0.29	0.78	0.43	-0.16	1.18	3.64

120

effects of financial assumption by regional or state governments is clearly to lower tax burdens on the poor—it can happen, but given the almost certainty of leveling-up effects and the political feasibility of always using state personal income taxes to finance the shifted amount it is not likely to happen.

Chapter Eight

Conclusions: The Policy Implications of Direct Financial Assumption

These case studies represent one of very few intensive efforts to measure the effects of state/regional government financial assumption. The results suggest a range of possible effects of direct financial assumption, but more importantly show that the equity results depend to a very great extent on how the reform is structured. This chapter is a brief summary of that range of effects, with a description of the features of an optimal version of direct assumption, with discussion of a set of other relevant considerations, and finally with some thoughts on the "selling" of this reform option. We conclude with a capsule review of the findings of this research.

EFFECTS

The policy theme of this research is that the clear advantages of fiscal centralization lie in potentially favorable equity effects. There are economic efficiency, technical efficiency, and short- and long-term cost effects, but these are extremely difficult to guage. If this contention holds, then direct state or regional government financial assumption, to be justified on equity grounds, ought to do at least four things: (1) it should lower the tax burdens on the urban poor; (2) it should provide some measure of relief to the central-city government; (3) it should reduce, if not eliminate, city/suburb disparities in tax burden; (4) it should result in a less regressive distribution of tax burdens across income classes. Under certain conditions the specific shifting programs proposed in these studies accomplish all of these objectives, a result which is clear from the comparative analysis presented in the preceding chapter. Under other conditions some of these goals are not accomplished.

By way of summary it might be useful to itemize the potential effects of the financial assumption alternative. First, it is clear that tax burdens on the urban poor can be reduced under fiscal centralization *if* the shift is from local property tax financing to state personal income tax financing. Particularly where the function shifted is education, increased use of state income taxation is almost essential to achieving this equity result. When the shift is to a regional government property tax or sales tax, the tax burden effects are generally lesser in magnitude and do not appear to provide marked relief to the urban poor.

Second, the shifting of financial responsibility, particularly for education and welfare, will provide considerable relief to the central-city fisc. This might happen in one or both of two ways. The shift of financial responsibility for a selected set of functions may free-up an amount of resources that had been used to support those functions, which then could be used to support other city-financed functions. These case studies suggest that declines in overall resident tax liability will not typically be the case. But even if the city government may not raise taxes, the city's fiscal position could benefit simply because of removal of a set of growing expenditure requirements from its domain.[a]

Third, if the state/regional government makes use of personal income taxation, overall vertical equity probably will be improved; that is, even if the tax burden on the poor does not fall, their *relative* tax burdens may be lower. If state or regional government assumption involved substitution of retail sales for property taxes, then the effects on the relative tax burdens of families in different income brackets would depend heavily on the local features of the two taxes—for instance on their exemptions for food, clothing, and the like under the sales tax, or whether there is some form of income tax rebate, homestead exemption, or preferential treatment of the elderly under the local property tax. In the case studies presented here, the general conclusion is that the state or regional sales tax is less regressive than the property tax, and therefore the lower income classes would benefit relatively more by a shift to sales tax financing, even after allowance for interregional exporting. Finally, in cases where a shift is proposed from a local property to a regional property tax, there is no reason (apart from the exporting question) to expect a change in the *relative* distribution of effective rates across income classes.

Fourth, though not directly addressed in this research, it would appear that state financial assumption would reduce central-city/outside-central-city tax burden disparities in the case of all functions except education. However, in the case of state financial assumption of education, it appears that the central-city proportion of total state education expenditures is generally less than the central-city proportion of the total income or sales tax base. In such a case the shift of education financing to the state results in the assumption by central-city residents of financial responsibility for a portion of what had been spent for that function in the rest of the state. As was shown in the case studies

---

[a]However, in some states where city governments have already reached the statutory tax rate limits, state/regional financial assumption will provide additional room for further property tax increments. In the long run, then, one might conclude that such action will raise the overall property tax burden on central-city residents and consequently on the poor.

above, this additional burden on city residents tends to disappear as the city's industrial structure permits it to export a greater proportion of property taxes and as the level of city education spending is approximately equal to, or less than, that in the balance of the state.

Fifth, because the plans proposed here suggest that relief to central-city residents will always come in the form of reduced property taxes, many of the benefits of fiscal centralization in any particular state will accrue to residents of other states; that is, as the taxes on "exporting" industries are reduced, and to the extent the property tax is shifted forward, these reduced tax benefits will be passed along to consumers in other states in the form of lower prices.[b] But a secondary effect of this price benefit to out-of-state residents is an improvement in the competitive position of local firms.

On the basis of the results reported in these case studies, one might make a reasonable guess about the aggregate effects of state/regional financial assumption. It would appear that leveling-up—either statewide or regionwide—is almost certain to occur, and in such a case the *level* of tax burdens on city residents will probably rise at all income levels. These tax burdens will rise relatively more at higher income levels, thereby improving the *relative*, if not the absolute, tax burden position of the poor. Yet, if the incidence of this program is to be considered in terms of both tax and expenditure effects, the poor may fare even better, since with the leveling-up effect an interjurisdictional equalization of service levels is likely to occur.

It is not clear, however, that service-level benefits will be a result of intrastate or intraregional equalization of spending levels. If leveling-up essentially results in raising public employee wage and fringe benefit levels, little by way of public-service improvement may result. If such wage rate increments do occur, the result would appear to be simply a transfer of income from taxpayers in general to public employees. Since in most of these case studies the poor experienced net tax increments per dollar of income, it is not at all clear that this transfer improves overall equity.

OPTIMAL DESIGN OF FINANCIAL ASSUMPTION

Without repeating the major issues or guidelines associated with a proper assignment of financing and delivery responsibility, it would seem useful to translate the lessons of these case studies into a set of rules for an optimal design of a state/regional government financial assumption program. In order to maximize the potential favorable effects of such reform on the fiscal position of the central-city government and the relative income position of the poor, the follow-

---

[b]On the other hand, if the property tax is shifted backwards, these benefits will accrue to the owners of capital, who in the case of "exporting" firms are also likely to reside out of state.

ing guidelines might be considered: (1) central-city government relief can be maximized by shifting those functions that account for a large portion of the budget, that are fast growing, that are not easily postponable, and that may be particularly responsive to increasing concentrations of the poor, such as education, welfare, and packages of related social services. In particular it would appear that cities may find considerable financial relief by considering packages of seemingly unrelated subfunctions for financial reassignment to higher levels of government; (2) the state or regional tax used to finance the higher level of expenditure assumed should be relatively (as compared to the local property tax) progressive—either personal income taxes or sales taxes which have a broad set of exclusions from the taxable base (food, clothing, drugs, and the like). Moreover, increments in existing state taxes such as personal income taxes, might be made in a progressive way, such as by increasing the marginal rates or adding more brackets with higher rates at the upper end of the scale; (3) the tax burden effect on central-city residents might be maximized by reducing only residential property taxes, since the reduction of all property taxes allows part of the benefits of state or regional government financial assumption to be shifted out of state in the form of lower prices of exported goods and services or in the form of higher returns to owners of capital who reside outside the state; and (4) if there is a leveling-up process that exerts an upward pressure on expenditures, there should be considerable attention given to redesigning service districts. This would insure a reassignment of public employees and physical equipment that would, in turn, equalize, or tend to equalize, actual servicing levels. The alternative form of leveling-up—an equalizing of wage rates, pension levels, fringe benefits, and so on—may do little to improve the relative level of services provided inside central cities.

SELLING FINANCIAL ASSUMPTION

Throughout the 1960s there was a continuing debate over the merits of proposed financial assumption, reassignment, or government reform measures. Proponents of these reforms have always leaned heavily on the argument of technical efficiency gains that would be realized, and the cost savings and implications of tax reduction to follow. But technical efficiencies from increased size of government operations have not been demonstrated, and it is virtually certain that costs will not fall in the short run. One could argue persuasively that the immediate effects of any financial centralization scheme will be to raise taxes.

The thesis here is that financial assumption is going to have to be justified, and sold, on equity grounds. It is clear from these results that a carefully designed program of financial assumption is capable of reducing tax burdens on the poor, improving the equity of the tax burden distribution among income classes, and reducing city/suburb disparities in overall tax burdens and expenditure levels. It is also clear that these equity gains cannot be made unless the reform program is designed to achieve these ends. Finally, it is clear that these equity gains will be made at the expense of certain losses: in local autonomy and in the form of increased taxes.

The selling of this reform, in the sense of a clear identification of its effects, would seem to call for the design of a program that would maximize the favorable equity consequences. The presentation of such a program should emphasize hard empirical estimates of the tax burden and service-level gains, and the contribution to softening the financial emergency of the city government.

All this is not to say that the existence of equity gains makes financial centralization programs politically feasible. Indeed, there is strong evidence that particularly state legislatures are not likely to be sold on reforms on the basis of equity. The point is that there is no other strong basis for recommending centralization. If it is to be sold at all, it must be on equity grounds.

SUMMARY

Over two decades of federal/state/local government reform actions have not eliminated the serious public-sector inequities that characterize urban America: lower service levels and higher tax burdens in central cities than in suburban areas, an overburden on the budget resources of city governments, and relatively high tax burdens on the urban poor. A combination of inflation, the bargaining successes of public employee unions, and the continuing decline of central-city economies has pushed the situation beyond crisis proportions, and suggests a reinforcing of these inequities.

The root of the equity problem is that central city governments have too much functional responsibility relative to their capacity to finance public services. That is, city governments simply do too much. To deal with this imbalance, it is clear that a shift in the financing and delivery of public services to higher-tier governments is necessary. The two most feasible forms of this shift would appear to be state financial assumption and the creation of regional financing districts.

Regional and state government financing is going to have to be justified on equity grounds. Properly formulated, such fiscal centralization schemes can result in reduced interjurisdictional disparities in tax burden and service levels, and an improvement in the overall progressivity of the tax system. Other effects of fiscal centralization, however, are less clear. It seems probable that with fiscal centralization locals will lose some control over the mix of services they get, major scale economies which lead to cost savings probably will not be realized, and at least short-run government costs will rise.

The nine Urban Observatory (UO) cities studied here—all metropolitan central cities—display wide variation in socioeconomic and demographic characteristics. For example, per capita income is one-third lower in Baltimore than in Denver; population density in the most crowded city (Boston) is nine times that of the least crowded (Kansas City, Missouri); and the proportion of the central-city population that is nonwhite ranges from 7 percent in San Diego to 51 percent in Baltimore. In spite of this wide variation, there are at least three basic trends that most of the nine cities share: (1) each city is becoming a less dominant force in the SMSA, despite annexation; (2) city residents are poorer than their suburban counterparts, and (3) central cities are gaining increasing concentrations of population groups that may place relatively high expenditure demands on local governments while generating relatively few resources.

The range of functions chosen for state or regional government assumption varies widely among the nine cities. Predictably, the functions considered most often are those that lie at the heart of the urban fiscal problem—education and welfare. However, an additional thirty subfunctions were suggested for state/regional assumption (see Table 4-1), suggesting the belief that cities provide a far greater range of services than is necessary.

To assess the equity of the present tax system in each of these nine cities, an inclusive definition of income was used, and similar assumptions were made about the incidence of major state and local government taxes. The results show highly regressive tax burden distributions for central-city residents (see Table 5-4 and 5-5).

In each city, the local staff studied the effects on this tax burden distribution of shifting the financing of certain functions to state/regional taxes—primarily state income, state sales, and regional property taxes. The exact form of this financing shift varies widely among the cities depending on the particulars of the state/local tax structure.

The results of the case study analyses reveal that state financial assumption can, and probably will, have positive effects on the *distribution* of tax burdens, by lowering the overall regressivity of the state/local tax system. However, these results also suggest that overall service costs will rise in the event of fiscal centralization. These findings hold in every study. The results are not so uniform with respect to a number of other possible effects of state financial assumption; specifically, about how centralization effects (1) the budgetary position of the central city; (2) the *level* of central-city resident tax burdens; and (3) interjurisdictional fiscal disparities.

In the case of state assumption of *education* financing, two conclusions emerge. First, the aggregate tax burden on central-city residents will probably increase, particularly in cities where central-city/outside-central-city disparities are great, the concentration of exporting industries in the central city is heavy and where substantial statewide "leveling-up" of expenditures will be required. In such cases resident tax liabilities could increase by as much as 50 percent. Second, even with these increases in aggregate tax liability, the tax burdens of lower income city families declines and that for higher income city families rises. The degree of this heightened progressivity of tax burdens depends on the state government tax that is used. Because of the increase in aggregate tax liability on city residents, the city government is not likely to experience substantial budgetary relief; that is, resources will not be freed-up for other uses. It should be emphasized that these favorable tax burden effects are largely the result of using the state income tax to finance increased state education costs.

The conclusions to be drawn from the two case studies of the impact of state assumption of *welfare* financing are: (1) central-city residents, in aggregate, will experience considerable tax relief; (2) the central-city government will receive budget relief by shifting the function, and conceivably some "free resources," that is *aggregate* tax liabilities could be maintained with an increase in local taxes; and (3) most central-city residents will experience decreases in effective tax rates depending on the state tax used, and the equity of the effective rate pattern will be improved, particularly if the state income tax is used.

For all other functions studied—which we refer to as the *service package*—three conclusions emerge. First, the amount of budget relief to be gained by central-city governments when the service package is shifted varies widely, and is not always substantial. Second, in aggregate, the tax liabilities of central-city residents decrease. Third, lower income central-city residents may experience tax decreases, but since sales and income taxes are generally proposed for regional shifts, their burden declines may be only slight, or they may even experience tax increases.

If the reforms proposed here were undertaken in all nine cities, it would, indeed, be a sweeping change in intergovernmental financing arrangements in these nine states. Assuming for the moment that such a change were politically feasible, the pattern of tax burden distribution—both among jurisdictions within the state and among families in different income classes—would be markedly altered. There would, as well, be a substantial relief of pressures on the core-city budget. In short, state assumption would improve interjurisdictional and interpersonal equity in tax burdens and might tend to equalize service levels, but it would probably raise overall tax burdens on central-city residents.

By way of an overview of the potential effects of the financial assumption alternative, five results might be generalized. First, it is clear that tax burdens on the urban poor can be reduced under fiscal centralization *if* the shift is from local property tax financing to state personal income tax financing. Particularly where the function shifted is education, increased use of state income taxation is almost essential to achieving this equity result. When the shift is to a regional government property tax or sales tax, the tax burden effects are generally lesser in magnitude and do not appear to provide marked relief to the urban poor.

Second, the shifting of financial responsibility, particularly for education and welfare, will provide considerable relief to the central-city fisc. This might happen in one or both of two ways. The shift of financial responsibility for a selected set of functions may free up an amount of resources that had been used to support those functions, and which then could be used to support other city-financed functions. These case studies suggest that declines in resident tax liability, which results in freed resources, will not typically be the case. But even if the city government may not raise taxes, the city's fiscal position could benefit simply because of removal of a set of growing expenditure requirements from its domain.

Third, if the state/regional government makes use of personal income taxation, overall vertical equity probably will be improved; that is, even if the tax burden on the poor does not fall, their *relative* tax burdens may be lower. If state or regional government assumption involved substitution of retail sales for property taxes, then the effects on the relative rax burdens of families in different income brackets would depend heavily on the local features of the two taxes—for example, on their exemptions for food, clothing, and so on, under the sales tax, whether there is some form of income tax rebate, homestead exemption, or preferential treatment of the elderly under the local property tax. In the case studies presented here, the general conclusion is that the state or regional sales tax is less regressive than the city property tax and, therefore, the lower income classes would benefit relatively more by a shift to sales-tax financing—even after allowance for interregional exporting. Finally, in cases where a shift is proposed from a local property to a regional property tax, there is not reason (apart from the exporting question) to expect a change in the *relative* distribution of effective rates across income classes.

Fourth, though not directly addressed in this research, it would appear that state financial assumption would reduce central-city/outside-central-city tax burden disparities in the case of all functions except education. However, in the case of state financial assumption of education, it appears that the central-city proportion of total state education expenditures is generally less than the central-city proportion of the total income or sales-tax base. In such a case, the shift of education financing to the state results in the assumption by central-city residents of financial responsibility for a portion of what had been spent for education by local governments in the rest of the state. This additional burden on city residents tends to disappear as the city's industrial structure permits it to export a greater proportion of property taxes and as the level of city education spending is approximately equal to, or less than, that in the balance of the state.

Fifth, because the plans proposed here suggest that relief to central-city residents will always come in the form of reduced property taxes, many of the benefits of fiscal centralization in any particular state will accrue to residents of other states; that is, as the taxes on "exporting" industries are reduced, and to the extent the property tax is shifted forward, these reduced tax benefits will be passed along to consumers in other states in the form of lower prices.

However, a secondary effect of this price benefit to out-of-state residents is an improvement in the competitive position of local firms.

On the basis of these results, one might make a reasonable estimate of the aggregate effects of state/regional financial assumption in other cities. It would appear that a leveling-up—either statewide or regionwide—is almost certain to occur, and in such a case the *level* of tax burdens on city residents will probably rise at all income levels. However, these tax burdens will rise relatively more at higher income levels, thereby improving the *relative,* if not the absolute, tax burden position of the poor. However, if the incidence of this program is to be considered in terms of both tax and expenditure effects, the poor may fare even better, since with the leveling-up effect, an interjurisdictional equalization of service levels is likely to occur. It is not clear, however, that service-level benefits will be a result of intrastate or intraregional equalization of spending levels. If leveling-up essentially results in raising public employee wage and fringe benefit levels, little by way of public service improvement may result. If such wage rate increments do occur, the result would appear to be simply a transfer of income from taxpayers to public employees. Since in most of these case studies the poor experienced net tax increments per dollar of income, it is not at all clear that this transfer improves overall equity.

It would seem appropriate to conclude with a reemphasis of the importance of the property tax incidence assumptions to the results of this study. If, as the "new view" would hold the property tax is shifted backwards, then there are not significant equity gains to be had from likely forms of state financial assumptions. The forward shifting assumption made here would seem justifiable on two counts: the focus here on a central city in an SMSA where property taxation is not uniform; and the fact that we are dealing with relatively small tax changes in a relatively small sector of the economy hence capital markets are not likely to be significantly affected. To the extent these arguments do not hold up, the equity dimensions of state and regional government financial assumption are a different story from the one told here.

Appendix A

Industry Codes[a]

City		LAFFS	LMINS	LCONS	LMFCS	LFLWS	LPRMS	LFBMS	LNEMS	LEMSS	LTRQS	LODGS	LFKPS	LTXTS
Atlanta	SMSA[b]	29.7	18.6	105.7	78.5	86.0	22.7	44.7	32.1	43.7	191.3	75.5	94.5	91.6
	CC[c]	71.5	15.8	106.9	70.6	102.2	23.4	37.0	23.3	22.7	114.2	83.4	106.5	113.2
	OCC[d]	15.0	17.1	95.9	80.0	66.9	21.7	47.9	35.6	53.4	225.1	70.5	86.7	78.3
Boston	SMSA	20.8	7.5	82.4	89.2	44.9	11.6	67.5	100.9	162.5	75.5	106.4	68.8	76.5
	CC	30.8	6.3	82.2	73.9	46.9	12.4	65.2	58.6	87.7	50.3	81.6	84.7	118.4
	OCC	11.5	6.4	73.1	89.5	40.4	11.2	66.2	108.2	117.8	79.4	111.7	63.2	61.4
Baltimore	SMSA	45.9	12.4	102.2	100.2	68.6	182.8	75.4	60.4	128.5	94.5	104.5	95.7	91.3
	CC	49.3	11.9	118.5	140.5	97.4	287.0	106.7	58.6	128.0	146.8	148.9	144.6	151.3
	OCC	32.5	11.5	86.1	70.7	50.6	93.6	52.5	61.5	129.1	62.0	71.2	57.3	51.2
Denver	SMSA	51.9	138.0	101.3	67.7	47.2	17.0	89.6	66.1	59.6	62.0	83.1	103.1	21.8
	CC	80.2	172.0	95.6	63.2	75.5	16.9	66.8	43.3	44.0	44.4	67.2	99.2	32.3
	OCC	33.1	111.7	97.8	69.5	29.2	16.6	104.7	80.9	70.1	73.9	93.9	104.7	14.7
Kansas City[e]	SMSA	51.3	31.3	93.6	90.6	44.4	56.3	101.5	59.6	119.7	99.6	87.1	88.4	56.6
	CC	68.1	40.1	96.9	89.3	45.4	49.3	88.9	46.2	118.7	96.2	106.4	81.7	73.9
	OCC	33.6	26.4	85.7	90.5	41.9	60.0	108.2	67.5	119.8	101.8	74.8	93.1	46.3
Milwaukee	SMSA	44.2	13.3	70.9	139.8	36.6	152.1	167.2	338.9	212.3	89.5	111.4	134.5	36.5
	CC	47.1	8.7	67.5	146.8	29.5	139.7	151.9	317.7	227.1	125.2	128.0	144.4	52.6
	OCC	35.5	15.8	71.5	132.8	42.4	159.5	183.2	367.3	203.5	61.8	94.1	122.1	22.1
Nashville-Davidson	SMSA	68.3	13.0	110.2	93.9	139.6	10.5	81.7	28.5	33.8	89.2	95.2	87.1	170.6
	CC	71.4	12.6	115.3	89.1	107.3	9.7	70.2	27.1	36.7	86.2	88.3	84.2	160.2
	OCC	119.1	22.2	127.0	128.3	289.6	12.3	138.2	41.9	31.6	135.2	131.3	98.4	256.5
San Diego	SMSA	95.8	14.7	107.9	69.8	41.7	4.7	152.3	47.4	90.0	203.6	58.2	39.5	33.2
	CC	145.0	13.2	93.7	74.8	39.3	2.9	195.3	51.1	93.1	223.1	55.3	37.9	37.9
	OCC	68.3	15.4	116.6	64.8	45.3	6.6	108.8	45.0	89.4	196.4	61.4	40.9	29.3

City		LPRPS	LCHMS	LONDS	LRRES	LTRWS	LCOMS	LUTSS	LWHTS	LFBDS	LEDRS	LGMRS	LMVRS	LORTS
Atlanta	SMSA	113.7	65.9	77.5	94.1	153.2	141.1	111.9	163.0	82.0	78.4	149.1	96.2	96.8
	CC	98.7	65.0	85.6	96.5	171.6	113.4	112.7	136.2	63.7	96.0	124.7	75.3	96.0
	OCC	132.9	62.0	65.8	95.2	137.4	166.0	111.3	183.1	91.9	69.0	174.4	101.3	101.7
Boston	SMSA	148.1	55.2	98.1	34.2	78.6	130.8	86.1	113.7	109.6	99.3	107.8	59.2	101.8
	CC	151.4	43.6	78.5	48.3	79.8	133.7	91.3	98.3	96.6	108.5	95.4	42.2	85.9
	OCC	159.5	51.4	79.6	30.7	73.4	138.6	84.8	122.6	113.2	99.5	121.2	59.5	113.9
Baltimore	SMSA	124.9	110.9	79.9	104.0	101.8	95.4	109.6	96.1	99.9	88.6	111.9	75.5	87.5
	CC	151.5	155.1	112.4	130.5	137.7	105.6	150.3	116.8	137.6	109.3	131.6	75.0	103.4
	OCC	107.4	86.2	52.1	83.9	75.1	90.4	76.2	80.9	71.9	70.9	98.6	73.8	75.8
Denver	SMSA	114.9	46.5	86.7	87.8	124.5	125.1	93.4	138.3	91.4	116.5	109.8	102.9	96.4
	CC	115.1	45.8	108.3	103.3	111.5	126.5	91.0	140.0	84.2	115.2	102.9	91.7	96.1
	OCC	120.9	45.7	65.3	76.8	129.0	129.1	94.7	139.6	97.1	117.9	121.0	106.9	99.6
Kansas City*	SMSA	188.6	102.0	90.2	192.1	161.9	102.6	99.3	153.7	82.8	84.6	123.9	100.9	105.5
	CC	172.2	90.4	99.4	141.1	155.0	97.3	98.7	137.9	72.3	88.5	111.2	99.1	106.9
	OCC	215.6	102.2	82.9	234.5	159.9	112.4	99.2	169.9	90.2	82.7	141.3	99.5	109.1
Milwaukee	SMSA	147.3	51.6	85.0	65.4	102.3	77.5	95.5	107.2	104.9	106.2	127.0	70.5	87.3
	CC	144.8	60.9	99.9	75.4	117.2	78.6	101.5	99.6	101.3	105.7	126.6	65.6	82.7
	OCC	155.0	46.9	65.2	54.0	87.5	77.9	87.1	116.8	109.8	104.6	129.5	75.0	93.7
Nashville-Davidson	SMSA	232.1	141.8	117.5	72.7	139.8	119.8	103.8	131.6	92.3	76.0	104.3	99.4	90.3
	CC	246.5	176.0	96.3	80.5	155.4	121.4	91.6	138.6	91.5	75.7	104.0	103.6	85.3
	OCC	113.0	136.6	202.6	28.4	111.2	92.4	148.7	89.6	100.8	59.6	80.0	112.2	94.2
San Diego	SMSA	88.9	20.1	19.9	7.6	47.9	120.8	91.9	78.4	96.4	132.2	114.0	112.9	107.0
	CC	88.3	27.7	19.4	8.0	40.7	115.7	83.7	75.1	88.0	129.5	100.7	102.7	98.8
	OCC	92.4	15.5	18.8	7.1	54.4	129.7	99.8	82.9	106.0	132.7	133.4	122.5	117.9

City		LBPRS	LIRES	LBSUS	LRSUS	LPUHS	LOPSS	LPRSS	LPADS	LENRS	LHOSS	LNHHS	LEOTS	LEDGS
Atlanta	SMSA	143.6	157.1	157.4	115.7	124.0	106.5	122.6	105.4	87.4	63.7	90.5	78.0	74.5
	CC	137.4	137.2	158.5	114.8	200.5	145.6	124.4	103.4	88.9	68.7	88.5	82.3	81.6
	OCC	153.3	175.0	165.8	113.1	69.8	82.4	125.9	104.2	90.3	66.6	97.4	80.2	72.6
Boston	SMSA	141.5	162.4	162.2	86.0	49.1	79.3	181.1	101.6	81.7	132.3	121.3	107.4	73.2
	CC	153.6	186.8	164.0	85.3	38.7	91.7	159.6	119.8	89.0	171.3	101.2	90.2	56.4
	OCC	145.2	162.6	173.8	83.7	59.5	87.1	202.7	94.7	84.6	136.6	119.2	121.4	80.5
Baltimore	SMSA	100.3	106.4	113.4	93.1	94.5	77.2	116.1	170.8	101.2	114.3	81.3	85.2	84.9
	CC	124.4	130.5	134.4	110.7	128.9	98.2	129.6	172.3	118.3	148.3	105.4	99.7	98.5
	OCC	81.9	85.4	99.3	77.7	56.2	56.2	104.1	164.0	88.3	83.0	63.1	75.8	76.3
Denver	SMSA	125.3	143.6	159.9	112.1	59.7	100.6	133.2	114.1	125.1	115.5	113.4	103.7	105.0
	CC	129.5	148.0	154.1	117.7	62.0	109.3	126.5	110.9	119.3	137.2	115.1	85.9	80.5
	OCC	125.1	141.1	171.9	105.2	57.4	92.3	140.5	113.0	133.7	98.7	117.1	124.6	127.1
Kansas City*	SMSA	119.0	140.0	123.6	99.9	53.9	94.1	132.3	105.5	93.7	91.0	81.0	69.6	66.4
	CC	103.8	134.7	130.2	112.0	62.4	105.0	139.9	124.0	76.4	106.6	76.2	58.5	55.1
	OCC	135.6	147.8	125.6	90.2	47.2	86.7	131.4	91.9	90.7	105.3	93.0	77.7	69.5
Milwaukee	SMSA	94.7	107.2	110.4	75.0	43.4	72.8	98.6	68.8	94.1	106.4	110.6	80.2	74.4
	CC	96.5	99.4	106.7	75.6	37.7	72.1	86.7	78.6	84.8	97.8	98.8	70.2	65.5
	OCC	93.1	114.8	117.2	72.6	48.9	69.7	110.9	54.1	105.8	118.7	128.8	95.9	86.4
Nashville-Davidson	SMSA	119.5	136.0	106.5	103.3	123.0	110.0	86.9	85.5	109.2	128.1	91.3	90.5	67.9
	CC	116.2	136.4	109.5	106.9	103.0	102.2	83.9	88.3	106.5	120.8	90.1	94.5	69.5
	OCC	113.0	87.6	69.0	88.8	138.4	84.4	57.5	55.6	91.6	79.3	76.6	61.5	61.3
San Diego	SMSA	112.0	118.8	139.9	114.8	91.5	127.0	138.7	151.0	173.1	80.7	134.6	109.9	121.7
	CC	113.5	115.9	152.8	112.9	82.5	118.8	148.4	148.5	164.4	77.4	127.5	109.9	125.4
	OCC	110.7	119.7	125.6	114.3	98.1	131.7	118.5	146.4	183.8	84.8	146.5	112.3	120.4

City		LEDPS	LEDOS	LNPOS
Atlanta	SMSA	87.5	90.1	102.4
	CC	87.0	89.1	97.6
	OCC	95.4	96.7	111.9
Boston	SMSA	208.6	153.6	104.6
	CC	185.0	167.2	129.8
	OCC	242.0	161.7	108.9
Baltimore	SMSA	85.5	98.4	94.0
	CC	106.4	122.8	114.2
	OCC	70.2	80.8	77.4
Denver	SMSA	98.9	128.7	106.3
	CC	103.8	139.3	107.0
	OCC	100.4	125.5	101.6
Kansas City*	SMSA	78.3	112.6	101.6
	CC	68.3	110.2	101.9
	OCC	94.8	129.8	107.9
Milwaukee	SMSA	96.8	97.5	94.1
	CC	85.3	104.1	88.2
	OCC	115.1	90.9	98.8
Nashville-Davidson	SMSA	157.2	122.2	134.4
	CC	165.6	127.7	126.7
	OCC	54.2	65.6	91.3
San Diego	SMSA	70.6	130.4	115.4
	CC	71.9	136.1	107.9
	OCC	70.4	125.5	121.1

[a]For explanation, see "Industry Codes," p. 138, below.
[b]Standard Metropolitan Statistical Area.
[c]Central-city.
[d]Outside-central-city.
[e]Kansas and Missouri.

Industry Codes: Census Breakdown

Industry	Industry Code
Agriculture, forestry, and fisheries	AFF
Mining	MIN
Construction	CON
Manufacturing	MFG
Furniture and lumber and wood products	FLW
Metal industries (primary and fabricated)	PRM, FBM
Nonelectrical machinery	NEM
Electrical machinery, equipment, and supplies	EMS
Transportation equipment	TRQ
Other durable goods	ODG
Textile and allied products	TXT
Food and kindred products	FKP
Printing, publishing, and allied industries	PRP
Chemicals and allied products	CHM
Other nondurable goods (including not specified mfg. industries)	OND
Railroads and railway express service	RRE
Trucking and service warehousing	TRW
Other transportation	OTR
Communications	COM
Utilities and sanitary services	UTS
Wholesale trade	WHT
Food, bakery, and dairy stores	FBD
Eating and drinking places	EDR
General merchandise retailing	GMR
Motor vehicle retailing and service stations	MVR
Other retail trade	ORT

Industry Codes: Census Breakdown (continued)

Industry	Industry Code
Banking and credit agencies	BPR
Insurance and real estate	IRE
Business services and other repair services	BSU, RSU
Private households	PVH
Other personal services, and entertainment, recreation	OPS, ENR
Hospitals	HOS
Health services, except hospital	NHH
Elementary, secondary schools, and colleges = government (& total)	EDG, EDT
Elementary, secondary schools, and colleges = private (& other)	EDP, EDO
Welfare, religious, and nonprofit membership organizations	NPO
Legal, engineering, and miscellaneous professional services	PRS
Public administration	PAD

Appendix B

This appendix presents the methodology necessary to compute the level of "economic" income in the city, and to cross-classify this income by income class and family size. Eight steps are required:

1. The aggregation of available census income data into four classes: (1) wages and salaries; (2) proprietors income; (3) property income; and (4) transfer payments.
2. The distribution of income from these four sources among income classes.
3. An iterative technique necessary to correct for the distributional assumptions made in step two.
4. The correction of census data for underreporting.
5. The addition of capital gains.
6. The division of the SMSA income matrix into the central city and outside central city.
7. The redistribution of families among income classes to conform to the family income added to census income in steps 1 through 5 above.
8. The distributing of total families in each income class by size of family.

Through step 5, only the SMSA geographic unit is used. Thus for steps 1 through 5 above only two vectors exist: one for families in the SMSA, and one for unrelated individuals in the SMSA. After the operations of step 6, each of these two vectors is subdivided into a central-city matrix and an outside-central city matrix.

AGGREGATION OF INCOME DATA

The concept of income used in this analysis is as comprehensive a definition of income as could be developed for measurement purposes, since the objective is to estimate the tax burden imposed on total available resources. Such a comprehensive definition of income includes not only actual monetary income received by an individual, but also such items as the imputed rent from owner-occupied houses and also certain "fringe benefits" received by individuals but not included in money income.

The income data used in this study were obtained from the 1970 Census, the Department of Commerce, and the Internal Revenue Service. Since each of these organizations uses different definitions of income, it was necessary to combine the Census data in a manner so as to make it comparable to Commerce (OBE) data.

Data Sources

The Census provides data for six basic classes of income, separately for families and unrelated individuals. These are: (1) wages and salaries (WS); (2) nonfarm proprietorship (NFP); (3) farm proprietorships (FP); (4) Social Security (SS); (5) public assistance (PA); and (6) all other (O). For each of these sources, estimates are provided of the mean for each source, M_j, and the number of units receiving income from that source, n_j.

Let:

M_j = the mean income for the jth source for families

N_j = the number of families earning income from the jth source

M'_j = the mean income for the jth source for unrelated individuals

N'_j = the number of unrelated individuals earning income from the jth source

then the aggregate income for families for any one source (y_j) is:

$$y_j = (M_j)(N_j) \qquad (B-1)$$

and the aggregate income for unrelated individuals for any one source is:

$$y' = (M_j')(N_j') \qquad (B-2)$$

This data for M_j, M_j', N_j', N_j is provided in Table 89 of the Census fourth count, *General Social and Economic Characteristics by SMSA*. Table 89 also provides the number of families or unrelated individuals in each of fifteen income brackets.[1]

OBE Data

The Office of Business Economics provides annual data for four sources for *both* families and unrelated individuals combined. These classes are:

(1) wages and salary, (2) proprietors' income, (3) property income, and (4) transfer payments. This data is provided as a total for each source.[a,2]

Comparability of Census Data with OBE Data

Since Census and OBE data are based on different definitions, it was necessary to manipulate the components of income so as to make comparisons possible. The six categories reported by the Census can be combined in a manner that does not sacrifice information of economic content but does make them comparable to OBE data sources. The four comparable income sources that may be formed are (1) wages and salary (WS); (2) proprietors' income (PR); (3) property income (PTY); and (4) transfer income (TR). The following transformations were performed to obtain these four classes of income for each metropolitan area:

1. Wages and salaries were not altered.
2. Nonfarm proprietorship (NFP) and farm proprietorship (FP) were summed to proprietor income (PR).
3. Social Security (SS), and public assistance (PA), were added. Further it was estimated that, for the United States as a whole, these two items represent approximately 71.08 percent of total transfer income. Therefore, the SMSA data was divided by 0.7108 to yield total SMSA transfer income (TR).

$$TR = \frac{SS + PA}{0.7108} \qquad \text{(B-3)}$$

4. So as to maintain the original total income for the six sources combined, the amount by which the original sum of Social Security plus public assistance was increased to become transfer income, (TR) was then subtracted from the category "other income." This decision is based on the observation that the Census reports a sizable portion of transfer income under the category "other income" (O). After removal of this transfer income from the category "other income," what is left is earned from property income (PTY):

$$PTY = O - \left(\frac{SS + PA}{0.7108} - SS + PA \right) \qquad \text{(B-4)}$$

These operations are summarized below;

(1) $WS = WS$

(2) $PR = NFP + FP$

---

[a]Two minor adjustments were made to this data. The OBE amount for labor income was added to the category (1) wages and salaries, and personal contributions for social insurance were omitted.

(3) $TR = \dfrac{SS + PA}{0.7108}$

(4) $PTY = O - \left(\dfrac{SS + PA}{0.7108} - SS + PA \right)$

The four new sources of data are hereafter referred to as SC_i for Census data and SE_i for OBE data. To maintain the dichotomy of families and unrelated individuals, Census data is denoted as SC_i^f for families and SC_i^u for unrelated individuals.

DISTRIBUTION OF SOURCE INCOMES
AMONG INCOME CLASSES

Once the four source incomes (SC_i) for the Census were determined for both families and unrelated individuals, the next step was to distribute these source incomes among income classes. From Table 5 of the *Current Population Reports,*[3] the percent distribution of United States income by source, among income classes, was obtained.
Let:

US_{ij} = the percent of income earned in the nation in class i for
source j, where

$$i = 1, \ldots, 14; j = 1, \ldots, 4$$

The product of US_{ij} and the amount of income earned in the SMSA for the jth source yields the amount of income in class i for the jth source, or

$$SC_i^f = (US_{ij})(SC_j^f) \tag{B-5}$$

$$SC_{ij}^u = (US_{ij})(SC_j^u) \tag{B-6}$$

This provides two 4-by-14 matricies with the four rows showing income sources and the fourteen columns showing income classes. These are hereafter referred to as $[SC_{ij}]^f$ for families and $[SC_{ij}]^u$ for unrelated individuals.
The above procedure involves the assumption that source income, SC_j, in the SMSA is distributed among income classes in the same manner as income in the United States is distributed among income classes. This, of course, is a dangerous assumption, and a check seemed necessary. Such a check is the subject of the next section.

INTERATION OF THE MATRIX

In order to check the validity of the assumption presented in the preceding section, the following procedure was followed. From the matrix $[SC_{ij}]$ compute the row totals, RSC_{ij} (totals from any one income class), where

$$RSC_i = \sum_{j}^{4} SC_{ij}$$

It was reasoned that if the SMSA income is distributed among income classes exactly as U.S. source income is, then the mean computed for the ith class should be equal to the U.S. mean for the ith class. Since data are available for both the U.S. means by income class and the number of families or individuals in the SMSA in each income class, the U.S. class means can be compared with computed SMSA class means. Comparison of the U.S. income class means with the computed means should reveal that the U.S. and SMSA source incomes are not distributed in a similar manner.

In order to modify the original distribution in the matrix $[SC_{ij}]$ so as to bring the computed SMSA class means into line with the U.S. means, an iterative technique was devised.

Let:

(1) SC_j = SMSA income for the SMSA by source

(2) SC_{ij} = SMSA income for the ith class and jth source

(3) $RSC_j = \sum_{j}^{4} SC_{ij}$ total income in the ith class in the SMSA

(4) $TOT = \sum_{i}^{14} RSC_i$ total income of i classes in the SMSA

   or $TOT = \sum_{j}^{4} SC_j$ total income across j sources in the SMSA

(5) F_i = number of families in the ith class in the SMSA

(6) USM_i = U.S. mean income for ith class

(7) $FY_i = (F_i)(USM_i)$ = total income in the ith class of the SMSA if the SMSA and U.S. means are equal

(8) $USTOT = \sum_{j}^{14} FY_i$ total income in all i classes of SMSA if the SMSA and U.S. means are equal

(9) $TOT = \sum_{j}^{4} SC_j = USTOT$

The SMSA source income SC_j and TOT are considered control totals since they were taken from the SMSA Census data. The iterative procedure changes the distribution of these totals among the i income classes, but in the final matrix does not alter the distribution of the total (TOT) among the four source incomes (SC_j).

If it is assumed that the SMSA and U.S. have identical means for the ith income class, then the income in any one class of the SMSA is equal to the U.S. mean, USM_i, times the number of units in the ith class of the SMSA, or

$$FY_i = F_i * USM_i$$

Under this assumption the total income in the SMSA is $USTOT$, where

$$\sum_i^{14} FY_i = USTOT$$

The ratio $\dfrac{TOT}{USTOT}$ indicates the degree by which this procedure for estimating total SMSA income differs from the known SMSA source income TOT. Multiplying the ratio $\dfrac{TOT}{USTOT}$ by the vector FY_i yields a vector K such that:

$$K_i = \frac{TOT}{USTOT}\ FY_i \tag{B-7}$$

where:

$$TOT = \sum_i^{14} K_i \qquad i = 1, \ldots, 14.$$

Since FY_i is the amount of income in the ith class if the U.S. mean were equal to the SMSA mean, then K_i equals this amount, proportioned so that $\sum_j^{14} K_i$ must equal TOT, the SMSA source total. The goal of the iterative process is to obtain the respective K_i for each income class while maintaining the integrity of the original source totals SC_j.

The iterative technique is carried out in the following manner. For iterations on rows a vector β^1 is computed such that any β_i is:

$$\beta_i^1 = \frac{K_i}{RSC_i} \tag{B-8}$$

where $i = 1, \ldots, 14$

Multiplying this vector times each column of the original $[SC_{ij}]$ matrix yields

$$[SC_{ij}]^1 = \beta^1\ [SC_{ij}] \tag{B-9}$$

Summing down columns of the matrix $[SC_{ij}]^1$ yields new source totals, SC_j^1. These new source totals are the basis for iterations on columns. Summing SC_j^1 across the j sources yields the original source total TOT, but now the distribution among the four source incomes has changed. Thus, $SC_j^1 \neq SC_j^1$. Extending the procedure to iterations on columns acts to redistribute source income so that SC_j^2 approaches SC_j. To do this, a vector λ is constructed such that for any λ_j

$$\lambda_j = \frac{SC_j}{SC_j^1} \tag{B-10}$$

where $j = 1, \ldots, 4$

Multiplying this vector λ times the matrix $[SC_{ij}]^1$ yields $[SC_{ij}]^2$. The new row totals are

$$RSC_i^2 = \sum_j^4 SC_{ij}^2$$

This step completes one cycle of the interative procedure. The row-iterative procedure is repeated by replacing the denominator of β^1 with the new row totals RSC_i^2, or

$$\beta_i^2 = \frac{K_i}{RSC_i^2} \tag{B-11}$$

or for the ith iteration

$$\beta_i^r = \frac{K_i}{RSC^r} \tag{B-11a}$$

Thus, the row iterations always result in the new row totals approaching K_i. Similarly, the column-iterative procedure is repeated by always replacing the denominator of λ with the new column totals such that for any column iterations (c):

$$\lambda_j^c = \frac{SC_j}{SC_j^c} \tag{B-12}$$

where c = the number of the iteraction

Thus, the column iterations always approach SC_j as a limit. After each cycle (one row and one column iteration) the new row and column totals were compared to the original row and column total, respectively. When RSC_i^r was within 0.1 percent of K_i, and SC_j^c within 0.1 percent of SC_j, the iterative procedure was stopped. The iterative procedure can be presented more considely as follows.

Row Iterations

The procedure iterates toward row totals equal to K_i and source totals equal to SC_j.

Cycle 1

Row iterations are performed with a vector β such that

$$\beta_i^{\ 1} = \frac{K_i}{RSC_i}$$

and

$$\beta_i^{\ 1}\ [SC_{ij}] = [SC_{ij}]^2$$

Column iterations are performed with a vector λ such that

$$\lambda_j^{\ 1} = \frac{SC_j}{SC_j^1}$$

where

$$SC_j^{\ 1} = \overset{14}{\underset{i}{\Sigma}}[SC_{ij}]^1$$

and

$$\lambda_j^{\ 2}\ [SC_{ij}]^1 = [SC_{ij}]^2$$

Cycle 2

$$\beta^2 = \frac{K_i}{RSC_i^2}$$

where

$$RSC_i^{\ 2} = \Sigma\ [SC_{ij}]^2$$

and

$$\beta^2\ [SC_{ij}]^2 = [SC_{ij}]^3$$

and

$$\beta^2\ [SC_{ij}]^2 = [SC_{ij}]^3$$

$$\lambda^2 = \frac{SC_j}{SC_j^3}$$

where

$$SC_j^3 = \sum_j^{14} [SC_{ij}]^3$$

Cycle n

$$\beta^n = \frac{K_i}{RSC_i^n}$$

where

$$RSC_i^n = \sum_1^4 [SC_{ij}]^n$$

and

$$\beta^n [SC_{ij}]^n = [SC_{ij}]^{(n+1)}$$

$$\lambda^n = \frac{SC_j}{SC_j^{(n+1)}}$$

where

$$SC_j^{(n+1)} = \sum_1^{14} [SC_{ij}]^{(n+1)}$$

and

$$\lambda_j^n [SC_{ij}]^{(n+1)} = SC_{ij}^{(n+2)}$$

The completion of the iteration process yields a matrix $[SC_{ij}]^n$ such that SMSA source incomes originally distributed as U.S. source incomes were distributed but corrected to reflect the information provided by the U.S. class means.

CORRECTING THE LEVEL OF INCOME IN THE SMSA

The total income in the matrix $[SC_{ij}]^n$ is that provided from the four source incomes from the 1969 Census data. There is believed to be considerable under-reporting in Census income for the four sources, SC_j, as well as complete omission of a fifth source, capital gains. To correct for this, the four census source incomes were compared to the four OBE source incomes. Each of the OBE source incomes is larger than its corresponding Census source income, indicating that the OBE sources are more inclusive.[b] Thus, for each of the four sources a ratio was constructed such that

$$R_j = \frac{SOBE_j}{SC_j^F + SC_j^u} \qquad \text{(B-13)}$$

Multiplication of each ratio R_j times the corresponding jth column of tha matrix $[SC_{ij}]^n$ yields a new matrix, $[SC_{ij}]^A$, which corrects for the under reporting of income by the Census.

CORRECTION FOR THE OMISSION OF CAPITAL GAINS

The final correction for the level of income in the SMSA is to add capital gains income, which is completely omitted from the census income data. Two pieces of information were available to complete this operation. First, from Internal Revenue Service data the approximate amount of capital gains in the SMSA was available. Long-term gains in the excess of short-term losses was used to approximate the amount of capital gains in the metropolitan area. Since IRS uses Adjusted Gross Income as a base, the actual figure has to be doubled, since only one-half of long-term capital gains are taxable.

  A second useful component of available IRS data is the amount of capital gains realized in each income class in the United States. However, IRS income classes are adjusted gross income (AGI), whereas Census income classes are gross income. It is therefore necessary to adjust the amount of capital gains income in each IRS income class to conform with Census income classes. It has been estimated that AGI represents approximately 87 percent of gross income across all income classes,[4] and these estimates were used to make the appropriate adjustment, that is, it was assumed that this ratio holds equally for any income class. The U.S. percent distribution of capital gains income before and after adjustment is presented in Table B-1.[c]

---

[b]Before a comparison can be made, it is necessary to add together the Census family and individual source total, since OBE source totals are for both families and individuals.

[c]Specifically, the IRS data are adjusted in the following manner:
Let:

A_i = amount of capital gains in bracket i from IRS (where income is defined on an adjusted gross income concept)

G_i = amount of capital gains in bracket i (where income in bracket is defined on a gross basis)

Since it is known that

G_i = $0.87 A_i$

Table B-1. Percent Distribution of Capital Gains Before and After Adjustment for Class Definition

Income Class	I.R.S. Adjusted Gross Income Classes	Census Gross Income Classes
$0 - 999	0.0003%	0.0003%
1000 - 1999	0.0036	0.0037
2000 - 2999	0.0064	0.0061
3000 - 3999	0.0103	0.0097
4000 - 4999	0.0147	0.0142
5000 - 5999	0.0156	0.0156
6000 - 6999	0.0168	0.0167
7000 - 7999	0.0190	0.0187
8000 - 8999	0.0189	0.0189
9000 - 9999	0.0223	0.0218
10000 - 11999	0.0360	0.0342
12000 - 14999	0.0540	0.0517
15000 - 24999	0.1307	0.1208
over 25000	0.6514	0.6684

Capital gains data as provided by the IRS make no distinction between families and unrelated individuals. So in order to maintain the same distinction between families and unrelated individuals as is made in the balance of this study, total capital gains is partitioned into these two recipient classes. In order to partition capital gains in this fashion, a proxy variable was used. It was assumed that the division of property income (PTY) into that received by families, and by unrelated individuals would suitably approximate the proportions of capital gains earned by families and by unrelated individuals. The percent of property income (PTY) allocated to families and to unrelated individuals was computed from the Census income data. These proportions were then applied to the aggregate capital gains in the SMSA to derive separate estimates of the distribution of capital gains for families and unrelated individuals.

Let C^f and C^u equal the amount of capital gains for families and unrelated individuals respectively, and let the percent of distribution of capital

Then $G_{(i + 1)}$ = the amount of capital gains originally recorded as A'_i which should have been recorded as $G(i + 1)$

where

$$G_{(i + 1)} = (A_i - G_i) = 0.13 A_i$$

For any one bracket, the amount of capital gains income left in bracket $(i + 1)$ after adjustment is CG where

$$CG_{(i + 1)} = 0.87 A_{(i + 1)} + 0.13 A_i$$

The results of this process are shown in Table B-1.

gains among income classes (for families and individuals) be represented by P where any element, P_i is the percent of capital gains in income class i for families or unrelated individuals. Multiplying C^f times the vector P yields a vector of capital gains for families where the amount of capital gains for families in any one class i is:

$$C_i^f = P_i C^f \qquad (B-14)$$

where $\qquad\qquad i = 1, 1 \ldots , 14$

Similarly, for unrelated individuals, the amount of capital gains in any one class i is:

$$C_i^u = P_i C^u \qquad (B-15)$$

where $\qquad\qquad i = 1, \ldots , 14$

The amount of capital gains in each class for families was then added to the matrix $[SC_{ij}]_A^F$ as a fifth source column. This forms a new 14-by-5 matrix for families $[SC_{ij}]_{A+C}^F$. Similarly, a new matrix, $[SC_{ij}]_{A+C}^u$ was computed for unrelated individuals. Hereafter $[SC_{ij}]_{A+C}^F$ and $[SC_{ij}]_{A+C}^u$ are simply referred to as $[SC_{ij}]^F$ and $[SC_{ij}]^u$, respectively.

DISAGGREGATION OF THE METROPOLIAN
AREA INCOME MATRIX INTO CENTRAL-CITY
AND OUTSIDE-CENTRAL-CITY COMPONENTS

To this point, all estimates derived may be presented in two matrixes, one for families in the SMSA and one for unrelated individuals in the SMSA. Since the focus of this research is on the central city, the SMSA matrixes are disaggregated. The family matrix for the SMSA was subdivided into a family matrix for the central city and a family matrix for outside the central city. Similarly, the SMSA matrix for unrelated individuals was subdivided into a central-city portion and an outside-central-city portion. For convenience of presentation, the distinction between families and unrelated individuals is dropped temporarily, and only the geographic distinction SMSA, central city, and outside central city is observed.

The number of persons (families) in each income class in the SMSA matrix is divided into a central-city portion and an outside-central-city portion on the basis of the number of persons residing in the respective geographic unit. For each class the proportion of SMSA residents residing in the central city was calculated and used to apportion SMSA income. This process can be formalized as follows:

Let:

P = a column vector of fourteen elements such that P_i is the percent of all persons in the SMSA residing in the central city, *in income class i.*

$(1 - P)$ = a column vector of fourteen elements such that $(1 - P_i)$ is the percent of all persons in the SMSA residing outside the central city, *in income class i.*

Then the estimated matrix for the central city *(cc)* is:

$$P[SC_{ij}] = [SC_{ij}]_{cc} \qquad \text{(B-16)}$$

The matrix for outside the central city *(occ)* is:

$$(1 - P) [SC_{ij}] - [SC_{ij}]_{occ} \qquad \text{(B-17)}$$

Hereafter, for ease of presentation the distinction between city and suburbs will be dropped.

UPGRADING OF PERSONS AND INCOME BY CLASS

Correcting for underreporting of income data by the census, and inclusion of capital gains data, resulted in the addition of so much new income to each income class that the new class means lie above the original upper boundary of the class.

Specifically, dividing the row total for class i, RSC_i, by the number of families in class i, F_i yields a new mean, M_i'. M_i' is always greater than M_i and in most cases M_i' is greater than the upper boundary of income class i.

This implies that had the Census reported income data more fully and included capital gains, then many of the people (families) placed in income class i would have been placed in some higher income class. Similarly, if these individuals were actually in income class $(i + 1)$, $(i + 2)$, or $(i + 3)$, then the incomes they earned should also been recorded in income class $(i + 1)$, $(i + 2)$ or $(i + 3)$. To adjust for this improper distribution of people and income among income classes, a technique for the "bumping-up" of income and people was devised. This technique relies on several simplifying assumptions.

Assume first that the units are distributed within any one income class in a rectangular fashion. Given a rectangular distribution it follows that U, the proportion of units below the adjusted mean M, can be shown to be:

$$U = \frac{b_2 - M_i}{b_2 - b_1} \qquad \text{(B-18)}$$

where:

U = the proportion of units below the unadjusted mean

M_i = the unadjusted mean for class i

b_2 = the upper boundary of class i

b_1 = the lower boundary of class i

The above is appropriate for income classes 1–12. However, for income class 13 ($15,000–$25,000), it unusually large breadth makes a special method desirable. The method involves a special computation.[d]

Second, it is reasoned that since the adjusted mean (M_i) for any class i, has increased by a factor k_i, over the unadjusted mean (M_i) the boundaries must also be increased by the factor k_i. For example, if in the $2,000–3,000 class the original mean (M) was $2,474 and the adjusted mean (M^1) was $4,637, the ratio $\dfrac{M'_4}{M_4}$ = k_4 is 1.875, and it is assumed that the original b_1 = 3,000 and b_2 = 4,000 increased to B'_1 = (1.875) ($2,000) = $3,750, and B'_2 = (1.873) ($4,000) = $5,625. Thus, all the units (and income) that were originally noted to fall in the interval $2,000–3,000 are now assumed to lie in the interval $3,750 to $5,625. The only remaining problem is to estimate how many units, and similarly how much income falls in the $3,000–4,000 class versus $4,000–5,000 class versus the $5,000–6,000 class. Scrutiny of the M_i for any income class i revealed that four general types of outcomes are possible.

---

[d]We first standardize the distribution to be one unit in length. This is accomplished by determining the relative position of the unadjusted mean, $1_{M_1}{}^*$. So

$$M_1^* = \frac{m_1 - b_1}{b_2 - b_1} \tag{1}$$

We also assume a probability density function given by $(g - hx)$. It then follows that

$$\int_0^1 (g - hx)\, dx = 1 \tag{2}$$

$$\int_0^1 (g - hx)\, x\, dx = m_1 \tag{3}$$

$$\int_0^{m^*} 1 \, (g - hx)\, dx = \mu \tag{4}$$

Equation (1) defines a probability density function. Equation (2) defines the mean, while the final equation holds true under the assumption of uniformity, (1) and (2) can be solved for g and h, which then are substituted into (3) to determine U.

For demonstrative purposes, only one, the most complicated outcome, is discussed here. In this type outcome the new boundaries, B'_1 and B'_2 are such that three income classes are involved.

For example, in this case, part of the $3,000 to $4,000 class is overlapped by all of the $4,000 to $5,000 class as well as part of the $5,000 to $6,000 class (see Figure B-1). It is known that the number of families between b_1 and M_1 is $(U)A$. It is reasoned that the number of families between B_1 and M_1 is $(U)A$, and that the $(U)A$ families are evenly distributed between B_1 and

Class 4 (2,000–3,000)

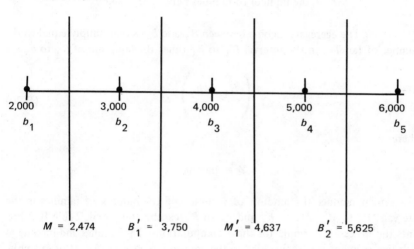

2,000	3,000	4,000	5,000	6,000
b_1	b_2	b_3	b_4	b_5

$M = 2,474$ $B'_1 = 3,750$ $M'_1 = 4,637$ $B'_2 = 5,625$

M_4 = unadjusted to mean

M'_4 = adjusted mean

$k_4 = \dfrac{M'_i}{M_1} = \dfrac{4,637}{2,474} = 1.873$

$B'_1 = k_4{}^*b_1 = \$3,000 = \$3,750$

$B'_2 = k_4{}^*b_2 = \$5,625$

U = percent of people below the original mean
$(1-u)$ = percent of people above the original mean
A = number of people in the class 2,000 to 4,000

Figure B-1. Adjustment of Number of Persons in $2000–$3000 Income class

M_1. The number of families between B'_1 and b_3 (in the \$3,000-\$4,000 class) can then be calculated as the ratio of the line segment $(B'_1 - b_3)$ to $(B'_1 - M'_1)$ times the number of families between B'_1 and M'_1 or:

$$F = \left(\frac{b_3 - B'_1}{M'_1 - B_1} \right) UA \qquad \text{(B-19)}$$

where:

$$F = \text{the number of families between } B'_1 \text{ and } b_3$$

The aggregate income between B'_1 and b_3 is then simply equal to the number of families in the interval B'_1 to b_3 times the midpoint of B'_1 to b_3 or:

$$Y \left(\frac{B'_1 + b_3}{2} \right) F \qquad \text{(B-20)}$$

where:

$$Y = \text{income}$$

In a similar manner the amount of income and the number of families in the intervals, b_3 to M'_1, M'_1 to b_4 and b_4 to B'_2 can be computed. Table B-2 presents the necessary formula for these computations. The families and income in each line segment was then added to the appropriate income class. For example, the number of families in line segment B'_1 to b_3 were assigned to the appropriate income class. The number of families in line segment B'_1 to b_3 were assigned to the income class \$3,000-\$4,000.

After shifting for each income class is accomplished, there remain only two steps to complete the distribution of income by income class and income type. The first is to allocate the shifted aggregate income across income types based on the proportion of total income form each income source in the original income class.

The second is then to sum all of these shifted amounts by source and compute new percent distributions across each income class. These final two steps can be formalized for any one income class i as follows:

Let:

$$P_j = \text{a vector of percents of length five such that } P_{ij} \text{ is the percent of total income in class } i \text{ from source } j \text{ before shifting has occurred.}$$

Table B-2. Formulae for Correcting for Number of Families in each Income Class

Interval	Income Class	Number of Families	Amount of Income
$B_1' \rightarrow b_3$	\$3,000–3,999	$\left(\dfrac{b_3 - \beta_1'}{M_1' - \beta_1'}\right)(UA)$	$\left[\left(\dfrac{b_3 - \beta_1'}{M_1' - \beta_1'}\right)(MA)\right]\left(\dfrac{\beta_1' + b_3}{2}\right)$
$b_3 \rightarrow M_1'$	\$4,000–4,999	$\left(\dfrac{M_1' - b_3}{M_1' - \beta_1'}\right)(UA)$	$\left[\left(\dfrac{M_1' - b_3}{M_1' - \beta_1'}\right)(MA)\right]\left(\dfrac{M_1' + b_3}{2}\right)$
$M_1' \rightarrow b_4$	\$4,000–4,999	$\left(\dfrac{b_4 - M_1'}{\beta_2' - M_1'}\right)(A - UA)$	$\left[\left(\dfrac{b_4 - M_1'}{\beta_2' - M_1'}\right)(A - UA)\right]\left(\dfrac{M_1' + b_4}{2}\right)$
$b_4 \rightarrow \beta_2$	\$5,000–5,999	$\left(\dfrac{\beta_2' - b_4}{\beta_2' - M_1'}\right)(A - UA)$	$\left[\left(\dfrac{\beta_2' - b_4}{\beta_2' - M_1'}\right)(A - UA)\right]\left(\dfrac{b_4 + \beta_2'}{2}\right)$

$P_j' = $ a vector of percents of length five such that P_{ij} is the percent of total income in class j from source j after shifting has occurred.

$P_{(i-1)} = $ a vector of length six so that $P_{(i-1), j}$ is the percent of total income in class $(i-1)$ from source j before any shifting has occurred.

$P_{(i-n)} = $ a vector of length six so that $P_{(i-n), j}$ is the percent of total income in class $(1-n)$ from source j before any shifting has occurred.

Let:

$Y_i' = $ the total of income in class i after the shifting has occurred.

Y_i = the amount of income left in class from class i after shifting has occurred.

$Y_{(i-1)}$ = the amount of income shifted into class i from class $(i-1)$.

$Y_{(i-n)}$ = the amount of income shifted into class i from class $(i-n)$.

Then the new percent distribution of aggregate income in class i after shifting is:

$$P_i = \frac{P_i Y_i + P_{(i-1)} Y_{(i-1)} + P_{(i-2)} Y_{(i-2)}, \ldots, P_{(i-n)} Y_{(i-n)}}{Y'_i} \quad \text{(B-21)}$$

The matrix $[P_{ij}]^*$, the percent distribution of income by source j, within each income class i, after the shifting process.

DISTRIBUTION BY FAMILY SIZE

One of the stated objectives of this work is to compute the tax burden on a tax-payer, incorporating the knowledge that the tax bill is a function of both the taxpayer's income class and the number of persons in that taxpayer's household. Obviously, for individuals the household size is one. However, family income data as gathered by the Census incorporates household sizes of from two persons to six or more persons. Therefore, before any tax bill can be computed for a tax-payer in the ith income class, the distribution of household size must be known for the ith class.

From Census data (Table 199 of the detailed count) the percent distribution of families by size of family within any one income class i was computed. However, this is the percent distribution of families before any shifting of families occurred. In order to derive the proper percent distribution of family size after shifting of families, it is necessary to go through a process similar to that carried on for the distribution of income across sources. The creation of a new percent distribution of families (by size) can be formalized as follows:

Let:

PF_i = a vector of percents of length 5 such that F_{ij} is the percent of the total families in class i of size j before shifting of families has occurred.

PF'_i = a vector of length 5 such that PF_{ij} is the percent of total families of size j after shifting of families has occurred.

$PF_{(i-1)}$ = a vector of length 5 such that $PF_{(i-1)}, j$ is the percent of total families in class $(i-1)$ of size j before any shifting has occurred.

$PF_{(i-n)}$ = a vector of length 5 such that $PF_{(i-n)}$, j is the percent of total families in class $(i-n)$ of size j before any shifting has occurred.

And let:

F'_i = the total number of families in class i after shifting has occurred.

F_i = the number of families left in class i from class i after shifting has occurred.

$F_{(i-1)}$ = the number of families shifted into class i from class $(i-1)$

$F_{(i-n)}$ = the number of families shifted into class i from class $(i-n)$

Then, the new percent distribution of families in class i after shifting is:

$$PF'_i = \frac{PF'^* F_i + PF_{(i-1)}* F_{(i-1)} + \ldots + PF_{(i-n)}^* F_{(i-n)}}{F'_i} \quad \text{(B-22)}$$

NOTES

1. U.S. Department of Commerce, Bureau of the Census, Census Fourth Count, *General Social and Economic Characteristics* (Washington, D.C.: Government Printing Office, 1970), Table 89.
2. U.S. Department of Commerce, Office of Business Economics, *Survey of Current Business* (Washington, D.C.: Government Printing Office, May 1971), p. 21.
3. U.S. Department of Commerce, Bureau of the Census, *Current Population Reports, Consumer Income 1969* (Washington, D.C.: Government Printing Office, 1970), Table 5.
4. John A Gorman, "The Relationship between Personal Income and Taxable Income," *Survey of Current Business* (May 1970), p. 19.

Appendix C

CENTRAL PROJECT DIRECTORS

Roy W. Bahl

Professor of Economics and Director, Metropolitan Studies Program, The Maxwell School of Citizenship and Public Affairs, Syracuse University, Syracuse, New York

Walter Vogt

Instructor of Economics, California State University, San Diego, California

CITY PROJECT DIRECTORS RESEARCH STAFF

National League of Cities:

Lawrence Williams

Program Administrator, National League of Cities, Washington, D.C.

Atlanta Urban Observatory:

David L. Sjoquist

Assistant Professor of Economics, Georgia State University, Atlanta, Georgia

Larry D. Schroeder

Assistant Professor of Economics, Georgia State University, Atlanta, Georgia

William H. Wilken — Assistant Professor of Political Science, Georgia State University, Atlanta, Georgia

Baltimore Urban Observatory:

William H. Oakland — Professor of Economics, Ohio State University, Columbus, Ohio

Eliyahu Borukhov — Lecturer, Department of Economics, Tel Aviv University, Tel Aviv, Israel

Milwaukee Urban Observatory:

Arthur P. Becker — Professor of Economics, University of Wisconsin at Milwaukee, Milwaukee, Wisconsin

Nashville Urban Observatory:

William A. Perry — University of Tennessee at Nashville, Nashville, Tennessee

Robert A. Horton — Director of Administration Analysis Division, Office of the Mayor, Nashville, Tennessee

J. Edmund Newman — Assistant Director of Administrative Analysis Division, Office of the Mayor, Nashville, Tennessee

San Diego Urban Observatory:

James D. Kitchen — Director, School of Public Administration and Urban Studies, California State University at San Diego, San Diego, California

W. Richard Bigger — Professor of Public Administration and Urban Studies, California State University at San Diego, San Diego, California

George Babilot

Professor of Economics, California State University at San Diego, San Diego, California

Boston Urban Observatory:

Joseph S. Slavet

University of Massachusetts at Boston, Boston, Massachusetts

Katherine Bradbury

Massachusetts Institute of Technology, Boston, Massachusetts

Philip Moss

Massachusetts Institute of Technology, Boston, Massachusetts

Denver Urban Observatory:

William O. Winter

University of Colorado

Chris H. Tomasides

City and County of Denver

James Adams

University of Colorado

John W. Richeson

City and County of Denver

Kansas City Urban Observatory:

Kenneth Hubbel

Associate Professor of Economics, University of Missouri, Kansas City, Missouri

Gerald Olsen

Assistant Professor of Economics, University of Missouri, Kansas City, Missouri

John Ward

Assistant Professor of Economics, University of Missouri, Kansas City, Missouri

Samuel Ramenofsky

Assistant Professor of Economics, University of Missouri, Kansas City, Missouri

Bibliography

Aaron, Henry, et al. "The Property Tax: Progressive or Regressive." *American Economic Review.* May 1974. pp. 212-235.

Aaron, Henry. *Shelters and Subsidies: Who Benefits from Federal Housing Policies?* Washington, D.C.: Brookings, 1972.

Aaron, Henry. *Who Pays the Property Tax?* Washington, D.C.: Brookings, 1975.

Advisory Commission on Intergovernmental Relations. *City Financial Emergencies: The Intergovernmental Dimension.* Washington, D.C.: ACIR, July 1973. Appendix B.

Advisory Commission on Intergovernmental Relations. *Financing Schools and Property Tax Relief: A State Responsibility; A Commission Report.* Washington, D.C.: ACIR, 1967.

Advisory Commission on Intergovernmental Relations. *Fiscal Balance in the American Federal System.* Vol. 2. Washington, D.C.: ACIR, 1967.

Advisory Commission on Intergovernmental Relations. *Government Functions and Processes: Local and Areawide.* Vol. IV in *Substate Regionalism and the Federal System.* Washington, D.C.: ACIR, 1974.

Advisory Commission on Intergovernmental Relations. *Performance of Urban Functions: Local and Areawide.* In *Substate Regionalism and the Federal System.* Washington, D.C.: ACIR, Sept. 1963. Appendix A.

Advisory Commission on Intergovernmental Relations. *State and Local Finances: Significant Features 1967 to 1970.* Washington, D.C.: ACIR, Nov. 1969.

Babilot, George; Bigger, W.R.; and Kitchen, James D. *Shifting Public Functions and the Distribution of Tax Burden by Economic Class: A Model and Empirical Observation.* San Diego, California: Urban Observatory of San Diego, June 1972.

Babilot, George; Bigger, W.R.; and Kitchen, James D. *A Study of Local Government Finance in the San Diego SMSA.* San Diego: San Diego Urban Observatory, June 1972.

165

Bahl, Roy W. "Louisville Intergovernmental Reforms for Fiscal Progress." *Fiscal Issues in the Future of Federalism.* Supplementary Paper No. 23. New York: Committee for Economic Development, May 1968.

Bahl, Roy W. *Metropolitan City Expenditures: A Comparative Analysis.* Lexington, Ky.: University of Kentucky Press, 1969.

Bahl, Roy W. "Public Policy and the Urban Fiscal Problem: Piecemeal vs. Aggregate Solutions." *Land Economics.* Feb. 1970. pp. 41-50.

Bahl, Roy W. and Campbell, Alan. "The Implications of Urban Government Reform: Efficiency, Equity, Cost and Administration Dimensions." *The Political Economy of Government Reform.* Eds. Roy Bahl and Alan Campbell. New York: Free Press, forthcoming.

Bahl, Roy W.; Campbell, Alan; and Greytak, David. *Taxes, Expenditures, and the Economic Base: A Case Study of New York City.* New York: Praeger, 1974.

Bahl, Roy W. and Gustely, Richard. "Wage Rates, Employment Levels and State and Local Government Expenditures for Health and Education: An Analysis of Interstate Variations." Ed. Selma J. Mushkin. State Aids for Human Services in a Federal System, Part II of *Services to People, State and National Urban Strategies.* Public Services Laboratory, Georgetown University, May 1974.

Bahl, Roy W. and Vogt, Walter. *Fiscal Centralization and Tax Burdens: State and Regional Financing of City Services.* Ballinger Press: forthcoming, 1976.

Bahl, Roy W. and Vogt, Walter. "The Fiscal Implications of Centralization." Working Paper No. 17. Maxwell Research Project on the Public Finances of New York City. Metropolitan Studies Program, Syracuse University, 1973.

Barzel, Yorham. "Two Propositions on the Optimum Level of Producing Public Goods." *Public Choice.* Spring 1961. pp. 31-37.

Becker, Arthur P. and Isakson, Hans Robert. "The Burden on the City of Milwaukee and Its Residents of the Real Property Tax Compared with the Income Tax." Paper presented at the Thirteenth Annual Conference of the Committee on Taxation. Resources and Economic Development, Madison, Wisconsin, October 25-27, 1974.

Becker, Arthur P. "Property Tax Reform: An Analysis of a Proposal for Milwaukee." *1974 Proceedings of the Sixty-Seventh Annual Conference on Taxation.* National Tax Association-Tax Institute of America. Columbus, Ohio, 1975.

Bish, Robert. *The Public Economy of Metropolitan Areas.* Chicago: Markham, 1971.

Bish, Robert and Ostrom, Vincent. *Understanding Urban Government.* Washington, D.C.: American Enterprise Institute, 1973.

Bradbury, Katherine; Moss, Philip; and Slavat, Joseph S. *Reallocation of Selected Municipal Services to the State: A Municipal Finance Alternative.* Boston, Mass.: The Boston Urban Observatory, October 1973.

Brazer, Harvey. *City Expenditures in the United States.* Occasional Paper 66. New York: National Bureau of Economic Research, 1959.

Break, George. "The Incidence and Effects of Taxation." *In Economics of Public Finance.* Washington, D.C.: Brookings, 1974. pp. 119-240.

Bureau of Public Affairs. *Impact of the State-Local Tax Services Mix on Municipal Finances in the Boston Metropolitan Area: A Preliminary Evaluation.* Boston, Mass.: The Boston Urban Observatory, 1972.

Campbell, Alan and Sacks, Seymour. *Metropolitan America; Fiscal Patterns and Government Systems.* New York: Free Press, 1967. Chap. 1.

Committee for Economic Development. *Fiscal Issues in the Future of Federalism.* Supplementary Paper No. 23. New York, New York: Committee for Economic Development, May 1968.

Coons, John E.; Clure, William H.; and Sugarman, Stephen D. *Private Wealth and Public Education.* Cambridge, Mass: Belknap Press of Harvard University Press, 1970. p. 202.

Cooper, Paul. "State Takeover of Education Financing." *National Tax Journal.* Sept. 1971. p. 350.

Dinkelmeyer, Robert and Greytak, David. "The Components of Change in New York City's Non-Labor Costs—Fiscal Year 1965-1970: Supplies, Materials, Equipment, And Contractual Services." Working Paper No. 13. Maxwell Research Project on the Public Finances of New York City. Syracuse, N.Y.: The Metropolitan Studies Program, Syracuse University, 1973.

Ehrenberg, Ronald. "The Demand for State and Local Government Employees." *American Economic Review.* June 1973. pp. 366-379.

Evans, James D. *Expenditure and Revenue Analysis: 1956-1971 for Metropolitan Nashville-Davidson County.* Nashville: Office of the Mayor, 1973.

Ferguson, Charles and Maurice, Charles. *Economic Analysis.* Homewood, Illinois: Richard D. Irwin, 1974.

Gorman, John A. "The Relationship between Personal Income and Taxable Income." *Survey of Current Business.* May 1970. p. 19.

Gramlich, Edward. "The Effect of Federal Grants on State-Local Expenditures: A Review of the Econometric Literature." *1969 Proceedings of the Sixty-Second Annual Conference on Taxation.* Boston, Mass: National Tax Association, 1970.

Gramlich, Edward M. and Galper, Harvey. "State and Local Fiscal Behavior and Federal Grant Policy." *Brookings Papers on Economic Activity 1.* 1973. pp. 15-65.

Greytak, David, et al. "The Effects of Inflation on Local Government Expenditures." *National Tax Journal.* Dec., 1974. pp. 583-598.

Greytak, David and Jump, Bernard. *The Impact of Inflation on the Expenditures and Revenues of Six Local Governments, 1971-1979.* Syracuse, N.Y.: The Metropolitan Studies Program, Syracuse University, June 1975.

Gustely, Richard. "Fiscal Equity, Efficiency and Government Consolidation." In *Evaluation of Two Tier Government: Case Studies of the Miami-Dade County Experience.* Vol. II. Eds. R. Langendorf and R. Stefbold. N.T.I.S. Springfield, Va., 1975.

Gustely, Richard. *Municipal Public Employment and Public Expenditure.* Lexington: Lexington Books, 1974.

Hirsch, Werner. "Cost Functions of an Urban Government Service: Refuse Collection." *Review of Economics and Statistics.* Feb. 1965. pp. 87-92.

Hubbell, K.; Olson, J.; Ramenossky, S.; and Ward, J. *Alternative Methods for Financing Public Services: The Cases of Education and Welfare, Kansas*

City, Missouri. Kansas City, Missouri: The Kansas City Urban Observatory, Aug. 1973.

Hubbell, Kenneth and Stephens, G. Ross. *Local Finance and Revenue-Sharing in the Kansas City SMSA, 1957 to 1980.* Kansas City, Mo.: Mid-America Urban Observatory, Aug. 1972.

Jump, Bernard. "Financing Public Employee Retirement Programs in New York City: Trends Since 1965 and Projections to 1980." Occasional Paper No. 16. Metropolitan Studies Program, The Maxwell School, Syracuse University, Jan. 1975.

Kee, Woo Sik. "Central City Expenditures and Metropolitan Areas." *National Tax Journal.* Dec. 1965. pp. 337-353.

Koleda, Michael. "A Public Good Model of Governmental Consolidation." *Urban Studies.* June 1971. pp. 103-110.

Merget, Astrid E. *The Expenditure Implications of Political Decentralization.* Working Paper No. 3. Maxwell Research Project on the Public Finances of New York City. Syracuse, New York: Metropolitan Studies Program, Syracuse University, 1973.

Mieszkowski, Peter. "The Property Tax: An Excise Tax or Profits Tax." *Journal of Public Economics.* Vol. 1. April 1972. pp. 73-96.

Musgrave, R.A., et al. "The Distribution of Tax Payments by Income Groups: A Case Study for 1948." *National Tax Journal.* March 1951. pp. 6-53.

Neenan, William B. *The Political Economy of Urban Areas.* Chicago: Markham Publishing Company, 1972.

Netzer, Dick. *Economics and the Urban Problems.* New York: Basic Books, 1970.

Oakland, William and Borukhov, Eliyahu. *Incidence and Other Fiscal Impacts of the Reform of Educational Finance: A Case Study of Baltimore.* Baltimore, Maryland: Baltimore Urban Observatory, Inc., April 1974.

Oakland, William; Borukhov, Eliyahu; Sparrow, Frederick T.; and Teplin, Albert. *Baltimore Municipal Finance Study.* Baltimore: Baltimore Urban Observatory, July 1972.

Oates, Wallace E. *Fiscal Federalism.* New York: Harcourt-Brace-Javanovich, 1972. Chap. 2.

Pechman, Joseph and Okner, Benjamin. *Who Bears the Tax Burden.* Washington, D.C.: Brookings, 1974.

Perry, William; Horton, Robert; and Newman, J. Edmund. *The Impact of State Assumption of Selected Metropolitan Nashville Expenditure Programs.* Nashville, Tennessee: The Urban Observatory of Metropolitan Nashville, Feb. 1974.

Phares, Donald. *State-Local Tax Equity: An Empirical Analysis of the Fifty States.* Lexington, Mass.: D.C. Heath and Company, 1973.

Sacks, Seymour and Callahan, John. *City Financial Emergencies: The Intergovernmental Dimension.* Vol. 2. The Advisory Commission on Intergovernmental Relations. Washington, D.C., 1967. Chap. 4.

Sacks, Seymour and Harris, Robert. "The Determinants of State and Local Government Expenditures and Intergovernmental Flows of Funds." *National Tax Journal.* March 1964. pp. 75-85.

Schroeder, Larry D.; Sjoquist, David L.; and Wilkens, William. *Spending and Tax Effects of Expanding Local Government Services Districts.* Atlanta: Atlanta Urban Observatory, March 1973.

Schroeder, Larry D.; Sjoquist, David L.; and Wilken, William H. *Shifting Public Service Functions: Expenditure-Revenue Effects on Political Feasibility.* Atlanta, Georgia: Atlanta Urban Observatory, April 1974.

Tucker, Rufus. "Distribution of Tax Burdens in 1948." *National Tax Journal.* Sept. 1971. p. 270.

U.S. Bureau of the Census. *Census of Population and Housing: 1970.* Series PHC (2): *General Demographic Trends for Metropolitan Areas,* 1960 to 1970.

U.S. Bureau of the Census. *Census of Population: 1970, Detailed Characteristics.* Final Report PC(1)-D1, *United States Summary.* Washington, D.C.: U.S. Government Printing Office, 1973.

U.S. Bureau of the Census. *City Government Finances in 1970-71.* Series GF71-No. 4. Washington, D.C.: U.S. Government Printing Office, 1972.

U.S. Department of Commerce, Bureau of the Census. *Current Population Reports, Consumer Income 1969.* Washington, D.C.: Government Printing Office, 1970. Table 5.

U.S. Department of Commerce, Bureua of the Census. *1970 Census Users Guide.* Washington, D.C.: U.S. Government Printing Office, 1970. pp. 108-109.

U.S. Department of Commerce, Bureau of the Census, Census, Fourth County. *General Social and Economic Characteristics.* Washington, D.C.: Government Printing Office, 1970. Table 89.

U.S. Department of Commerce, Bureau of the Census. *Local Government Employment in Selected Metropolitan Areas and Large Counties: 1965; 1973.* Washington, D.C.: Government Printing Office 1966; 1974.

U.S. Department of Commerce, Bureau of Economic Analysis. *Survey of Current Business.* Washington, D.C.: U.S. Government Printing Office, May 1971.

U.S. Department of Commerce, Office of Business Economics. *Survey of Current Business.* Washington, D.C.: Government Printing Office, May 1971. p. 21.

U.S. Treasury Department, Internal Revenue Service. *State and Metropolitan Area Data for Individual Income Tax Returns.* No. 471 (12-64) Washington, D.C.: U.S. Government Printing Office, 1964. pp. 10-14.

Winter, William; Tomasides, C.; Adams, J.; and Richeson, J. *Local Government Finance in the Denver Metropolitan Area, First Year Report.* Denver, Colorado: The Denver Urban Observatory, April 1972.

Winter, William; Tomasides, C.; Adams, J.; and Richeson, J. *Local Government Finance in the Denver Metropolitan Area, Second Year Report.* Denver, Colorado: The Denver Urban Observatory, Nov. 1973.

Index

ACIR (Advisory Commission on Intergovernmental Relations), 12; assignment criteria, 39; criteria in Denver, 80;
functional responsibility, 73
assessment, 21
Atlanta: profile, 27; regional financing,
114; regional government shift, 99;
regional payroll tax, 36
autonomy, 15; local and state assumption,
15

Baltimore: education and state assumption,
77; fiscal structure/trends, 34; increased
tax liability, 107; per capita income,
128; profile, 27; resident liability,
118; tax burden reduction, 118
Boston: aggregate tax liability, 118; fiscal
structure/trends, 34; function choice,
40; motor fuel tax allocation, 57; per
capita income, 128; profile, 27; and
property tax, 63; state financing, 114

capital: - labor substitution, 13
central city: and aggregate tax liability,
107; budget relief, 117; and concentration of poor, elderly, 27; disaggregation
of data, 152; expenditure disparity, 35;
fiscal profile, 9; infrastructure, 7; relief maximization, 126; relief and property taxes, 130; relief from centralization,
123; and shift scenario in Boston, 66,
67; tax relief, 124; tax relief and centralization, 112
centralization, 1, 12; and education spending, 15; effects, 123; and effect on low
incomes, 111; and income distribution,
61; state assumption of function, 19;
and target cities, 28; and welfare shift in
Milwaukee, 112

collective bargaining: centralization of, 19
Coons, J.E., Clurge, W.H. and Sugarman,
S.D., 15
costs: and regional financing districts, 20

Denver: per capita income, 128; profile,
27; property tax and welfare funding,
112; regional financing, 114; revenue-
expenditure gap, 79; welfare financing,
111

education: and aggregate tax liability, 107;
and central city resources, 11; financing
in target cities, 31; and fiscal crisis, 41;
and industrial/financial infrastructure,
130; in Kansas City, 68; San Diego, 73;
state assumption, 15, 76; state assumption in Baltimore, 78; state assumption
in Milwaukee, 97; tax shift and relief,
124; and urban fiscal problems, 128
efficiency: defined, 12; equity/service
delivery, 40; and shift scenario in Boston,
66, 67; and state/regional financial
assumption, 20
employment: levels, 35; and target cities,
31
equity: and central city problems, 127; and
centralization, 114, 123; defined, 15;
interpersonal 98, 111; interpersonal
effects of shift, 76; interpersonal and
state/regional financing, 17; and pro-
portionality, 73
expenditure: consequences, 39; and income redistribution, 111; on poor and
aged, 11; and redesigning service districts, 126; regressive taxes in Nashville,
86

financing: central city and tax relief,

171

About the Authors

Roy W. Bahl is Professor of Economics and Director, Metropolitan Studies Program in the Maxwell School of Syracuse University. He received his B.A. from Greenville College in 1961 and his Ph.D. from the University of Kentucky in 1965, and served on the faculty at West Virginia University and as an economist at the International Monetary Fund before coming to Syracuse University in 1971. He is the author of numerous books and articles on state and local finances including *Metropolitan City Expenditures: A Comparative Analysis* and *Taxes, Expenditures, and the Economic Base: A Case Study of New York City,* and has served widely as a consultant both in the United States and in a number of Developing Countries.

Walter Vogt is Assistant Professor of Economics at San Diego State University. He is also on the Committee for the Center of Public Economics at San Diego State. He received his B.A. from the State University of New York at Buffalo in 1967 and his Ph.D. from Syracuse University in 1975.